EQUITY ASSET VALUATION WORKBOOK

CFA Institute is the premier association for investment professionals around the world, with over 98,000 members in 133 countries. Since 1963 the organization has developed and administered the renowned Chartered Financial Analyst® Program. With a rich history of leading the investment profession, CFA Institute has set the highest standards in ethics, education, and professional excellence within the global investment community, and is the foremost authority on investment profession conduct and practice.

Each book in the CFA Institute Investment Series is geared toward industry practitioners along with graduate-level finance students and covers the most important topics in the industry. The authors of these cutting-edge books are themselves industry professionals and academics and bring their wealth of knowledge and expertise to this series.

EQUITY ASSET VALUATION WORKBOOK

Second Edition

Jerald E. Pinto, CFA

Elaine Henry, CFA

Thomas R. Robinson, CFA

John D. Stowe, CFA

with a contribution by

Raymond D. Rath, CFA

WILEY

John Wiley & Sons, Inc.

Published by John Wiley & Sons, Inc., Hoboken, New Jersey.
Published simultaneously in Canada.

For general information on our other products and services or for technical support, please contact our Customer
Care Department within the United States at (800) 762-2974, outside the United States at (317) 572-3993 or
fax (317) 572-4002.

Wiley also publishes its books in a variety of electronic formats. Some content that appears in print may not be
available in electronic books. For more information about Wiley products, visit our web site at www.wiley.com.

ISBN 978-0-470-39521-9

Printed in the United States of America.

10 9 8 7 6 5 4 3 2 1

CONTENTS

PART I

LEARNING OUTCOMES, SUMMARY OVERVIEW, AND PROBLEMS

CHAPTER 1

EQUITY VALUATION: APPLICATIONS AND PROCESSES

LEARNING OUTCOMES

After completing this chapter, you will be able to do the following:

- Define valuation and intrinsic value and explain two possible sources of perceived mispricing.
- Explain the going-concern assumption, contrast a going concern to a liquidation value concept of value, and identify the definition of value most relevant to public company valuation.
- List and discuss the uses of equity valuation.
- Explain the elements of industry and competitive analysis and the importance of evaluating the quality of financial statement information.
- Contrast absolute and relative valuation models and describe examples of each type of model.
- Illustrate the broad criteria for choosing an appropriate approach for valuing a particular company.

SUMMARY OVERVIEW

In this chapter, we have discussed the scope of equity valuation, outlined the valuation process, introduced valuation concepts and models, discussed the analyst's role and responsibilities in conducting valuation, and described the elements of an effective research report in which analysts communicate their valuation analysis.

- Valuation is the estimation of an asset's value based on variables perceived to be related to future investment returns, or based on comparisons with closely similar assets.
- The intrinsic value of an asset is its value given a hypothetically complete understanding of the asset's investment characteristics.
- The assumption that the market price of a security can diverge from its intrinsic value—as suggested by the rational efficient markets formulation of efficient market theory—underpins active investing.

- Intrinsic value incorporates the going-concern assumption, that is, the assumption that a company will continue operating for the foreseeable future. In contrast, liquidation value is the company's value if it were dissolved and its assets sold individually.
- Fair value is the price at which an asset (or liability) would change hands if neither buyer nor seller were under compulsion to buy/sell and both were informed about material underlying facts.
- In addition to stock selection by active traders, valuation is also used for
  - Inferring (extracting) market expectations.
  - Evaluating corporate events.
  - Issuing fairness opinions.
  - Evaluating business strategies and models.
  - Appraising private businesses.
- The valuation process has five steps:
  1. Understanding the business.
  2. Forecasting company performance.
  3. Selecting the appropriate valuation model.
  4. Converting forecasts to a valuation.
  5. Applying the analytical results in the form of recommendations and conclusions.
- Understanding the business includes evaluating industry prospects, competitive position, and corporate strategies, all of which contribute to making more accurate forecasts. Understanding the business also involves analysis of financial reports, including evaluating the quality of a company's earnings.
- In forecasting company performance, a top-down forecasting approach moves from macroeconomic forecasts to industry forecasts and then to individual company and asset forecasts. A bottom-up forecasting approach aggregates individual company forecasts to industry forecasts, which in turn may be aggregated to macroeconomic forecasts.
- Selecting the appropriate valuation approach means choosing an approach that is
  - Consistent with the characteristics of the company being valued.
  - Appropriate given the availability and quality of the data.
  - Consistent with the analyst's valuation purpose and perspective.
- Two broad categories of valuation models are absolute valuation models and relative valuation models.
  - Absolute valuation models specify an asset's intrinsic value, supplying a point estimate of value that can be compared with market price. Present value models of common stock (also called discounted cash flow models) are the most important type of absolute valuation model.
  - Relative valuation models specify an asset's value relative to the value of another asset. As applied to equity valuation, relative valuation is also known as the method of comparables, which involves comparison of a stock's price multiple to a benchmark price multiple. The benchmark price multiple can be based on a similar stock or on the average price multiple of some group of stocks.
- Two important aspects of converting forecasts to valuation are sensitivity analysis and situational adjustments.
  - Sensitivity analysis is an analysis to determine how changes in an assumed input would affect the outcome of an analysis.
  - Situational adjustments include control premiums (premiums for a controlling interest in the company), discounts for lack of marketability (discounts reflecting the lack of a public market for the company's shares), and illiquidity discounts (discounts reflecting the lack of a liquid market for the company's shares).

- Applying valuation conclusions depends on the purpose of the valuation.
- In performing valuations, analysts must hold themselves accountable to both standards of competence and standards of conduct.
- An effective research report
  - Contains timely information.
  - Is written in clear, incisive language.
  - Is objective and well researched, with key assumptions clearly identified.
  - Distinguishes clearly between facts and opinions.
  - Contains analysis, forecasts, valuation, and a recommendation that are internally consistent.
  - Presents sufficient information that the reader can critique the valuation.
  - States the risk factors for an investment in the company.
  - Discloses any potential conflicts of interest faced by the analyst.
- Analysts have an obligation to provide substantive and meaningful content. CFA Institute members have an additional overriding responsibility to adhere to the CFA Institute Code of Ethics and relevant specific Standards of Professional Conduct.

PROBLEMS

1. Critique the statement: "No equity investor needs to understand valuation models because real-time market prices for equities are easy to obtain online."

2. The text defined intrinsic value as "the value of an asset given a hypothetically complete understanding of the asset's investment characteristics." Discuss why "hypothetically" is included in the definition and the practical implication(s).

3. A. Explain why liquidation value is generally not relevant to estimating intrinsic value for profitable companies.
   B. Explain whether making a going-concern assumption would affect the value placed on a company's inventory.

4. Explain how the procedure for using a valuation model to infer market expectations about a company's future growth differs from using the same model to obtain an independent estimate of value.

5. Example 1-1, based on a study of Intel Corporation that used a present value model (Cornell 2001), examined what future revenue growth rates were consistent with Intel's stock price of $61.50 just prior to its earnings announcement, and $43.31 only five days later. The example states, "Using a conservatively low discount rate, Cornell estimated that Intel's price before the announcement, $61.50, was consistent with a forecasted growth rate of 20 percent a year for the subsequent 10 years and then 6 percent per year thereafter." Discuss the implications of using a higher discount rate than Cornell did.

6. Discuss how understanding a company's business (the first step in equity valuation) might be useful in performing a sensitivity analysis related to a valuation of the company.

7. In a research note on the ordinary shares of the Milan Fashion Group (MFG) dated early July 2007 when a recent price was €7.73 and projected annual dividends were €0.05, an analyst stated a target price of €9.20. The research note did not discuss how the target price was obtained or how it should be interpreted. Assume the target price represents the expected price of MFG. What further specific pieces of information would you need to form an opinion on whether MFG was fairly valued, overvalued, or undervalued?

8. You are researching XMI Corporation (XMI). XMI has shown steady earnings-per-share growth (18 percent a year during the past seven years) and trades at a very high multiple to earnings (its P/E is currently 40 percent above the average P/E for a group of the most comparable stocks). XMI has generally grown through acquisition, by using XMI stock to purchase other companies whose stock traded at lower P/Es. In investigating the financial disclosures of these acquired companies and talking to industry contacts, you conclude that XMI has been forcing the companies it acquires to accelerate the payment of expenses before the acquisition deals are closed. As one example, XMI asks acquired companies to immediately pay all pending accounts payable, whether or not they are due. Subsequent to the acquisition, XMI reinstitutes normal expense payment patterns.
   A. What are the effects of XMI's preacquisition expensing policies?
   B. The statement is made that XMI's "P/E is currently 40 percent above the average P/E for a group of the most comparable stocks." What type of valuation model is implicit in that statement?

CHAPTER 2

RETURN CONCEPTS

LEARNING OUTCOMES

After completing this chapter, you will be able to do the following:

- Distinguish among the following return concepts: holding period return, realized return and expected return, required return, discount rate, the return from convergence of price to intrinsic value (given that price does not equal value), and internal rate of return.
- Explain the equity risk premium and its use in required return determination, and demonstrate the use of historical and forward-looking estimation approaches.
- Discuss the strengths and weaknesses of the major methods of estimating the equity risk premium.
- Explain and demonstrate the use of the capital asset pricing model (CAPM), Fama-French model (FFM), the Pastor-Stambaugh model (PSM), macroeconomic multifactor models, and the build-up method (including bond yield plus risk premium method) for estimating the required return on an equity investment.
- Discuss beta estimation for public companies, thinly traded public companies, and nonpublic companies.
- Analyze the strengths and weaknesses of the major methods of estimating the required return on an equity investment.
- Discuss international considerations in required return estimation.
- Explain and calculate the weighted average cost of capital for a company.
- Explain the appropriateness of using a particular rate of return as a discount rate, given a description of the cash flow to be discounted and other relevant facts.

SUMMARY OVERVIEW

In this chapter we introduced several important return concepts. Required returns are important because they are used as discount rates in determining the present value of expected future cash flows. When an investor's intrinsic value estimate for an asset differs from its market price, the investor generally expects to earn the required return plus a return from the convergence of price to value. When an asset's intrinsic value equals price, however, the investor only expects to earn the required return.

For two important approaches to estimating a company's required return, the CAPM and the build-up model, the analyst needs an estimate of the equity risk premium. This chapter examined realized equity risk premia for a group of major world equity markets and also explained forward-looking estimation methods. For determining the required return on equity, the analyst may choose from the CAPM and various multifactor models such as the Fama-French model and its extensions, examining regression fit statistics to assess the reliability of these methods. For private companies, the analyst can adapt public equity valuation models for required return using public company comparables, or use a build-up model, which starts with the risk-free rate and the estimated equity risk premium and adds additional appropriate risk premia.

When the analyst approaches the valuation of equity indirectly, by first valuing the total firm as the present value of expected future cash flows to all sources of capital, the appropriate discount rate is a weighted average cost of capital based on all sources of capital. Discount rates must be on a nominal (real) basis if cash flows are on a nominal (real) basis.

Among the chapter's major points are the following:

- The return from investing in an asset over a specified time period is called the *holding period return*. *Realized return* refers to a return achieved in the past, and *expected return* refers to an anticipated return over a future time period. A *required return* is the minimum level of expected return that an investor requires to invest in the asset over a specified time period, given the asset's riskiness. The *(market) required return*, a required rate of return on an asset that is inferred using market prices or returns, is typically used as the *discount rate* in finding the present values of expected future cash flows. If an asset is perceived (is not perceived) as fairly priced in the marketplace, the required return should (should not) equal the investor's expected return. When an asset is believed to be mispriced, investors should earn a *return from convergence of price to intrinsic value*.
- An estimate of the equity risk premium—the incremental return that investors require for holding equities rather than a risk-free asset—is used in the CAPM and in the build-up approach to required return estimation.
- Approaches to equity risk premium estimation include historical, adjusted historical, and forward-looking approaches.
- In historical estimation, the analyst must decide whether to use a short-term or a long-term government bond rate to represent the risk-free rate and whether to calculate a geometric or arithmetic mean for the equity risk premium estimate. Forward-looking estimates include Gordon growth model estimates, supply-side models, and survey estimates. Adjusted historical estimates can involve an adjustment for biases in data series and an adjustment to incorporate an independent estimate of the equity risk premium.
- The CAPM is a widely used model for required return estimation that uses beta relative to a market portfolio proxy to adjust for risk. The Fama-French model (FFM) is a three factor model that incorporates the market factor, a size factor, and a value factor. The Pastor-Stambaugh extension to the FFM adds a liquidity factor. The bond yield plus risk premium approach finds a required return estimate as the sum of the YTM of the subject company's debt plus a subjective risk premium (often 3 percent to 4 percent).
- When a stock is thinly traded or not publicly traded, its beta may be estimated on the basis of a peer company's beta. The procedure involves unlevering the peer company's beta and then relevering it to reflect the subject company's use of financial leverage. The procedure adjusts for the effect of differences of financial leverage between the peer and subject company.
- Emerging markets pose special challenges to required return estimation. The country spread model estimates the equity risk premium as the equity risk premium for a developed market plus a country premium. The country risk rating model approach uses risk ratings for developed markets to infer risk ratings and equity risk premiums for emerging markets.

- The weighted average cost of capital is used when valuing the total firm and is generally understood as the nominal after-tax weighted average cost of capital, which is used in discounting nominal cash flows to the firm in later chapters. The nominal required return on equity is used in discounting cash flows to equity.

PROBLEMS

1. A Canada-based investor buys shares of Toronto-Dominion Bank (Toronto: TD.TO) for C\$72.08 on 15 October 2007, with the intent of holding them for a year. The dividend rate is C\$2.11 per year. The investor actually sells the shares on 5 November 2007, for C\$69.52. The investor notes the following additional facts:
   - No dividends were paid between 15 October and 5 November.
   - The required return on TD.TO equity was 8.7 percent on an annual basis and 0.161 percent on a weekly basis.
   A. State the lengths of the expected and actual holding periods.
   B. Given that TD.TO was fairly priced, calculate the price appreciation return (capital gains yield) anticipated by the investor given his initial expectations and initial expected holding period.
   C. Calculate the investor's realized return.
   D. Calculate the realized alpha.

2. The estimated betas for AOL Time Warner (NYSE: AOL), J.P. Morgan Chase & Company (NYSE: JPM), and The Boeing Company (NYSE: BA) are 2.50, 1.50, and 0.80, respectively. The risk-free rate of return is 4.35 percent and the equity risk premium is 8.04 percent. Calculate the required rates of return for these three stocks using the CAPM.

3. The estimated factor sensitivities of TerraNova Energy to Fama-French factors and the risk premia associated with those factors are given in the following table:

	Factor Sensitivity	Risk Premium (%)
Market factor	1.20	4.5
Size factor	−0.50	2.7
Value factor	−0.15	4.3

   A. Based on the Fama-French model, calculate the required return for TerraNova Energy using these estimates. Assume that the Treasury bill rate is 4.7 percent.
   B. Describe the expected style characteristics of TerraNova based on its factor sensitivities.

4. Newmont Mining (NYSE: NEM) has an estimated beta of −0.2. The risk-free rate of return is 4.5 percent, and the equity risk premium is estimated to be 7.5 percent. Using the CAPM, calculate the required rate of return for investors in NEM.

5. An analyst wants to account for financial distress and market capitalization as well as market risk in his cost of equity estimate for a particular traded company. Which of the following models is *most appropriate* for achieving that objective?

A. The capital asset pricing model (CAPM)

B. The Fama-French model

C. A macroeconomic factor model

6. The following facts describe Larsen & Toubro Ltd.'s component costs of capital and capital structure:

Component Costs of Capital	
Cost of equity based on the CAPM	15.6%
Pretax cost of debt	8.28%
Tax rate	30%
Target weight in capital structure	equity 80%, debt 20%

Based on the information given, calculate Larsen & Toubro's WACC.

Use the following information to answer Questions 7 through 12.

An equity index is established in 2001 for a country that has relatively recently established a market economy. The index vendor constructed returns for the five years prior to 2001 based on the initial group of companies constituting the index in 2001. Over 2004 to 2006 a series of military confrontations concerning a disputed border disrupted the economy and financial markets. The dispute is conclusively arbitrated at the end of 2006. In total, 10 years of equity market return history is available as of the beginning of 2007. The geometric mean return relative to 10-year government bond returns over 10 years is 2 percent per year. The forward dividend yield on the index is 1 percent. Stock returns over 2004 to 2006 reflect the setbacks but economists predict the country will be on a path of a 4 percent real GDP growth rate by 2009. Earnings in the public corporate sector are expected to grow at a 5 percent per year real growth rate. Consistent with that, the market P/E ratio is expected to grow at 1 percent per year. Although inflation is currently high at 6 percent per year, the long-term forecast is for an inflation rate of 4 percent per year. Although the yield curve has usually been upward sloping, currently the government yield curve is inverted; at the short end, yields are 9 percent and at 10-year maturities, yields are 7 percent.

7. The inclusion of index returns prior to 2001 would be expected to
   A. Bias the historical equity risk premium estimate upwards.
   B. Bias the historical equity risk premium estimate downwards.
   C. Have no effect on the historical equity risk premium estimate.

8. The events of 2004 to 2006 would be expected to
   A. Bias the historical equity risk premium estimate upwards.
   B. Bias the historical equity risk premium estimate downwards.
   C. Have no effect on the historical equity risk premium estimate.

9. In the current interest rate environment, using a required return estimate based on the short-term government bond rate and a historical equity risk premium defined in terms of a short-term government bond rate would be expected to

    A. Bias long-term required return on equity estimates upwards.

    B. Bias long-term required return on equity estimates downwards.

    C. Have no effect on long-term required return on equity estimates.

10. A supply-side estimate of the equity risk premium as presented by the Ibbotson-Chen earnings model is *closest* to

    A. 3.2 percent.

    B. 4.0 percent.

    C. 4.3 percent.

11. Common stock issues in this market with average systematic risk are *most likely* to have required rates of return

    A. Between 2 percent and 7 percent.

    B. Between 7 percent and 9 percent.

    C. At 9 percent or greater.

12. Which of the following statements is *most accurate*? If two equity issues have the same market risk but the first issue has higher leverage, greater liquidity, and a higher required return, the higher required return is most likely the result of the first issue's

    A. Greater liquidity.

    B. Higher leverage.

    C. Higher leverage and greater liquidity.

CHAPTER 3

DISCOUNTED DIVIDEND VALUATION

LEARNING OUTCOMES

After completing this chapter, you will be able to do the following:

- Compare and contrast dividends, free cash flow, and residual income as measures of cash flow in discounted cash flow valuation, and identify the investment situations for which each measure is suitable.
- Determine whether a dividend discount model (DDM) is appropriate for valuing a stock.
- Calculate the value of a common stock using the DDM for one-, two-, and multiple-period holding periods.
- Calculate the value of a common stock using the Gordon growth model and explain the model's underlying assumptions.
- Calculate the implied growth rate of dividends using the Gordon growth model and current stock price.
- Calculate and interpret the present value of growth opportunities (PVGO) and the component of the leading price-to-earnings ratio (P/E) related to PVGO, given no-growth earnings per share, earnings per share, the required rate of return, and the market price of the stock (or value of the stock).
- Calculate the justified leading and trailing P/Es based on fundamentals using the Gordon growth model.
- Calculate the value of noncallable fixed-rate perpetual preferred stock given the stock's annual dividend and the discount rate.
- Explain the strengths and limitations of the Gordon growth model and justify the selection of the Gordon growth model to value a company's common shares, given the characteristics of the company being valued.
- Explain the assumptions and justify the selection of the two-stage DDM, the H-model, the three-stage DDM, or spreadsheet modeling to value a company's common shares, given the characteristics of the company being valued.
- Explain the growth phase, transitional phase, and maturity phase of a business.
- Explain terminal value and discuss alternative approaches to determining the terminal value in a discounted dividend model.
- Calculate the value of common shares using the two-stage DDM, the H-model, and the three-stage DDM.

- Explain how to estimate a required return based on any DDM, and calculate that return using the Gordon growth model and the H-model.
- Define, calculate, and interpret the sustainable growth rate of a company, explain the calculation's underlying assumptions, and demonstrate the use of the DuPont analysis of return on equity in conjunction with the sustainable growth rate expression.
- Illustrate the use of spreadsheet modeling to forecast dividends and value common shares.

SUMMARY OVERVIEW

This chapter provided an overview of DCF models of valuation, discussed the estimation of a stock's required rate of return, and presented in detail the dividend discount model.

- In DCF models, the value of any asset is the present value of its (expected) future cash flows

$$V_0 = \sum_{t=1}^{n} \frac{CF_t}{(1+r)^r}$$

where V_0 is the value of the asset as of $t = 0$ (today), CF_t is the (expected) cash flow at time t, and r is the discount rate or required rate of return. For infinitely lived assets such as common stocks, n runs to infinity.
- Several alternative streams of expected cash flows can be used to value equities, including dividends, free cash flow, and residual income. A discounted dividend approach is most suitable for dividend-paying stocks in which the company has a discernible dividend policy that has an understandable relationship to the company's profitability, and the investor has a noncontrol (minority ownership) perspective.
- The free cash flow approach (FCFF or FCFE) might be appropriate when the company does not pay dividends, dividends differ substantially from FCFE, free cash flows align with profitability, or the investor takes a control (majority ownership) perspective.
- The residual income approach can be useful when the company does not pay dividends (as an alternative to an FCF approach) or free cash flow is negative.
- The DDM with a single holding period gives stock value as

$$V_0 = \frac{D_1}{(1+r)^1} + \frac{P_1}{(1+r)^1} + \frac{D_1 + P_1}{(1+r)^1}$$

where D_1 is the expected dividend at time 1 and V_0 is the stock's (expected) value at time 0. Assuming that V_0 is equal to today's market price, P_0, the expected holding period return is

$$r = \frac{D_1 + P_1}{P_0} - 1 = \frac{D_1}{P_0} + \frac{P_1 - P_0}{P_0}$$

- The expression for the DDM for any given finite holding period n and the general expression for the DDM are, respectively,

$$V_0 = \sum_{t=1}^{n} \frac{D_t}{(1+r)^t} + \frac{P_n}{(1+r)^n} \text{ and } V_0 = \sum_{t=1}^{\infty} \frac{D_t}{(1+r)^t}$$

- There are two main approaches to the problem of forecasting dividends. First, an analyst can assign the entire stream of expected future dividends to one of several stylized growth patterns. Second, an analyst can forecast a finite number of dividends individually up to a terminal point and value the remaining dividends either by assigning them to a stylized growth pattern or by forecasting share price as of the terminal point of the dividend forecasts.
- The Gordon growth model assumes that dividends grow at a constant rate g forever, so that $D_t = D_{t-1}(1+g)$. The dividend stream in the Gordon growth model has a value of

$$V_0 = \frac{D_0(1+g)}{r-g}, \text{ or } V_0 = \frac{D_1}{r-g} \text{ where } r > g$$

- The value of noncallable fixed-rate perpetual preferred stock is $V_0 = D/r$, where D is the stock's (constant) annual dividend.
- Assuming that price equals value, the Gordon growth model estimate of a stock's expected rate of return is

$$r = \frac{D_0(1+g)}{P_0} + g = \frac{D_1}{P_0} + g$$

- Given an estimate of the next-period dividend and the stock's required rate of return, the Gordon growth model can be used to estimate the dividend growth rate implied by the current market price (making a constant growth rate assumption).
- The present value of growth opportunities (PVGO) is the part of a stock's total value, V_0, that comes from profitable future growth opportunities in contrast to the value associated with assets already in place. The relationship is $V_0 = E_1/r + \text{PVGO}$, where E_1/r is defined as the no-growth value per share.
- The leading price-to-earnings ratio (P_0/E_1) and the trailing price-to-earnings ratio (P_0/E_0) can be expressed in terms of the Gordon growth model as, respectively,

$$\frac{P_0}{E_1} = \frac{D_1/E_1}{r-g} = \frac{1-b}{r-g} \text{ and } \frac{P_0}{E_0} = \frac{D_0(1+g)/E_0}{r-g} = \frac{(1-b)(1+g)}{r-g}$$

These expressions give a stock's justified price-to-earnings ratio based on forecasts of fundamentals (given that the Gordon growth model is appropriate).
- The Gordon growth model may be useful for valuing broad-based equity indexes and the stock of businesses with earnings that are expected to grow at a stable rate comparable to or lower than the nominal growth rate of the economy.
- Gordon growth model values are very sensitive to the assumed growth rate and required rate of return.
- For many companies, growth falls into phases. In the growth phase, a company enjoys an abnormally high growth rate in earnings per share, called supernormal growth. In the transition phase, earnings growth slows. In the mature phase, the company reaches an equilibrium in which such factors as earnings growth and the return on equity stabilize at levels that can be sustained long term. Analysts often apply multistage DCF models to value the stock of a company with multistage growth prospects.

- The two-stage dividend discount model assumes different growth rates in stage 1 and stage 2:

$$V_0 = \sum_{t=1}^{n} \frac{D_0(1+g_S)^t}{(1+r)^t} + \frac{D_0(1+g_S)^n(1+g_L)}{(1+r)^n(r-g_L)}$$

where g_S is the expected dividend growth rate in the first period and g_L is the expected growth rate in the second period.
- The terminal stock value, V_n, is sometimes found with the Gordon growth model or with some other method, such as applying a P/E multiplier to forecasted EPS as of the terminal date.
- The H-model assumes that the dividend growth rate declines linearly from a high super-normal rate to the normal growth rate during stage 1, and then grows at a constant normal growth rate thereafter:

$$V_0 = \frac{D_0(1+g_L)}{r-g_L} + \frac{D_0 H(g_S - g_L)}{r-g_L} = \frac{D_0(1+g_L) + D_0 H(g_S - g_L)}{r-g_L}$$

- There are two basic three-stage models. In one version, the growth rate in the middle stage is constant. In the second version, the growth rate declines linearly in stage 2 and becomes constant and normal in stage 3.
- Spreadsheet models are very flexible, providing the analyst with the ability to value any pattern of expected dividends.
- In addition to valuing equities, the IRR of a DDM, assuming assets are correctly priced in the marketplace, has been used to estimate required returns. For simpler models (such as the one-period model, the Gordon growth model, and the H-model), well-known formulas may be used to calculate these rates of return. For many dividend streams, however, the rate of return must be found by trial and error, producing a discount rate that equates the present value of the forecasted dividend stream to the current market price.
- Multistage DDM models can accommodate a wide variety of patterns of expected dividends. Even though such models may use stylized assumptions about growth, they can provide useful approximations.
- Dividend growth rates can be obtained from analyst forecasts, statistical forecasting models, or company fundamentals. The sustainable growth rate depends on the ROE and the earnings retention rate, b: $g = b \times \text{ROE}$. This expression can be expanded further, using the DuPont formula, as

$$g = \frac{\text{Net income} - \text{Dividends}}{\text{Net income}} \times \frac{\text{Net income}}{\text{Sales}} \times \frac{\text{Sales}}{\text{Total assets}} \times \frac{\text{Total assets}}{\text{Shareholders' equity}}$$

PROBLEMS

1. Amy Tanner is an analyst for a U.S. pension fund. Her supervisor has asked her to value the stocks of General Electric (NYSE: GE) and General Motors (NYSE: GM). Tanner wants to evaluate the appropriateness of the dividend discount model (DDM) for valuing GE and GM and has compiled the following data for the two companies for 2000 through 2007.

Year	GE			GM		
	EPS ($)	DPS ($)	Payout Ratio	EPS ($)	DPS ($)	Payout Ratio
2007	2.17	1.15	0.53	−68.45	1.00	−0.01
2006	1.99	1.03	0.52	−3.50	1.00	−0.29
2005	1.76	0.91	0.52	−18.50	2.00	−0.11
2004	1.61	0.82	0.51	4.94	2.00	0.40
2003	1.55	0.77	0.50	5.03	2.00	0.40
2002	1.51	0.73	0.48	3.35	2.00	0.60
2001	1.41	0.66	0.47	1.77	2.00	1.13
2000	1.27	0.57	0.45	6.68	2.00	0.30

Source: Compustat.

For each of the stocks, explain whether the DDM is appropriate for valuing the stock.

2. Vincent Nguyen, an analyst, is examining the stock of British Airways (London Stock Exchange: BAY) as of the beginning of 2008. He notices that the consensus forecast by analysts is that the stock will pay a £4 dividend per share in 2009 (based on 21 analysts) and a £5 dividend in 2010 (based on 10 analysts). Nguyen expects the price of the stock at the end of 2010 to be £250. He has estimated that the required rate of return on the stock is 11 percent. Assume all dividends are paid at the end of the year.
   A. Using the DDM, estimate the value of BAY stock at the end of 2009.
   B. Using the DDM, estimate the value of BAY stock at the end of 2008.

3. Justin Owens is an analyst for an equity mutual fund that invests in British stocks. At the beginning of 2008, Owens is examining domestic stocks for possible inclusion in the fund. One of the stocks that he is analyzing is British Sky Broadcasting Group (London Stock Exchange: BSY). The stock has paid dividends per share of £9, £12.20, and £15.50 at the end of 2005, 2006, and 2007, respectively. The consensus forecast by analysts is that the stock will pay a dividend per share of £18.66 at the end of 2008 (based on 19 analysts) and £20.20 at the end of 2009 (based on 17 analysts). Owens has estimated that the required rate of return on the stock is 11 percent.
   A. Compare the compound annual growth rate in dividends from 2005 to 2007 inclusive (i.e., from a beginning level of £9 to an ending level of £15.50) with the consensus predicted compound annual growth rate in dividends from 2007 to 2009, inclusive.
   B. Owens believes that BSY has matured such that the dividend growth rate will be constant going forward at half the consensus compound annual growth rate from 2007 to 2009, inclusive, computed in part A. Using the growth rate forecast of Owens as the constant growth rate from 2007 onwards, estimate the value of the stock as of the end of 2007 given an 11 percent required rate of return on equity.
   C. State the relationship between estimated value and r and estimated value and g.

4. During the period 1960–2007, earnings of the S&P 500 Index companies have increased at an average rate of 8.18 percent per year and the dividends paid have increased at an average rate of 5.9 percent per year. Assume that
   • Dividends will continue to grow at the 1960–2007 rate.
   • The required return on the index is 8 percent.
   • Companies in the S&P 500 Index collectively paid $27.73 billion in dividends in 2007.

Estimate the aggregate value of the S&P 500 Index component companies at the beginning of 2008 using the Gordon growth model.

5. Great Plains Energy is a public utility holding company that listed its 4.5 percent cumulative perpetual preferred stock series E on the NYSE Euronext in March 1952 (Ticker: GXPPrE). The par value of the preferred stock is $100. If the required rate of return on this stock is 5.6 percent, estimate the value of the stock.

6. German Resources is involved in coal mining. The company is currently profitable and is expected to pay a dividend of €4 per share next year. The company has suspended exploration, however, and because its current mature operations exhaust the existing mines, you expect that the dividends paid by the company will decline forever at an 8 percent rate. The required return on German Resource's stock is 11 percent. Using the DDM, estimate the value of the stock.

7. Maspeth Robotics shares are currently selling for €24 and have paid a dividend of €1 per share for the most recent year. The following additional information is given:
   • The risk-free rate is 4 percent,
   • The shares have an estimated beta of 1.2, and
   • The equity risk premium is estimated at 5 percent.

   Based on the above information, determine the constant dividend growth rate that would be required to justify the market price of €24.

8. You believe the Gordon (constant) growth model is appropriate to value the stock of Reliable Electric Corp. The company had an EPS of $2 in 2008. The retention ratio is 0.60. The company is expected to earn an ROE of 14 percent on its investments and the required rate of return is 11 percent. Assume that all dividends are paid at the end of the year.
   A. Calculate the company's sustainable growth rate.
   B. Estimate the value of the company's stock at the beginning of 2009.
   C. Calculate the present value of growth opportunities.
   D. Determine the fraction of the company's value which comes from its growth opportunities.

9. Stellar Baking Company in Australia has a trailing P/E of 14. Analysts predict that Stellar's dividends will continue to grow at its recent rate of 4.5 percent per year into the indefinite future. Given a current dividend and EPS of A$0.7 per share and A$2.00 per share, respectively, and a required rate of return on equity of 8 percent, determine whether Stellar Baking Company is undervalued, fairly valued, or overvalued. Justify your answer.

10. Mohan Gupta is the portfolio manager of an India-based equity fund. He is analyzing the value of Tata Chemicals Ltd. (Bombay Stock Exchange: TATACHEM). Tata Chemicals is India's leading manufacturer of inorganic chemicals, and also manufactures fertilizers and food additives. Gupta has concluded that the DDM is appropriate to value Tata Chemicals.

   During the past five years (fiscal year ending 31 March 2004 to fiscal year ending 31 March 2008), the company has paid dividends per share of Rs.5.50, 6.50, 7.00, 8.00, and 9.00, respectively. These dividends suggest an average annual growth rate in DPS of just above 13 percent. Gupta has decided to use a three-stage DDM with a linearly declining growth rate in stage 2. He considers Tata Chemicals to be an average growth company, and estimates stage 1 (the growth stage) to be 6 years and stage 2 (the transition stage) to be 10 years. He estimates the growth rate to be 14 percent in stage 1 and 10 percent in stage 3. Gupta has estimated the required return on equity for Tata Chemicals to be 16 percent. Estimate the current value of the stock.

11. You are analyzing the stock of Ansell Limited (Australian Stock Exchange: ANN), a health care company, as of late June 2008. The stock price is A\$9.74. The company's dividend per share for the fiscal year ending 31 June 2008 was A\$0.27. You expect the dividend to increase by 10 percent for the next three years and then increase by 8 percent per year forever. You estimate the required return on equity of Ansell Limited to be 12 percent.
    A. Estimate the value of ANN using a two-stage dividend discount model.
    B. Judge whether ANN is undervalued, fairly valued, or overvalued.

12. Sime Natural Cosmetics Ltd has a dividend yield of 2 percent based on the current dividend and a mature phase dividend growth rate of 5 percent per year. The current dividend growth rate is 10 percent per year, but the growth rate is expected to decline linearly to its mature phase value during the next six years.
    A. If Sime Natural Cosmetics is fairly priced in the marketplace, what is the expected rate of return on its shares?
    B. If Sime were in its mature growth phase right now, would its expected return be higher or lower, holding all other facts constant?

13. Kazuo Uto is analyzing the stock of Brother Industries, Ltd. (Tokyo Stock Exchange: 64480), a diversified Japanese company that produces a wide variety of products. Brother distributes its products under its own name and under original-equipment manufacturer agreements with other companies. Uto has concluded that a multistage DDM is appropriate to value the stock of Brother Industries and the company will reach a mature stage in four years. The ROE of the company has declined from 16.7 percent in the fiscal year ending in 2004 to 12.7 percent in the fiscal year ending in 2008. The dividend payout ratio has increased from 11.5 percent in 2004 to 22.3 percent in 2008. Uto has estimated that in the mature phase Brother's ROE will be 11 percent, which is approximately equal to estimated required return on equity. He has also estimated that the payout ratio in the mature phase will be 40 percent, which is significantly greater than its payout ratio in 2008 but less than the average payout of about 50 percent for Japanese companies.
    A. Calculate the sustainable growth rate for Brother in the mature phase.
    B. With reference to the formula for the sustainable growth rate, a colleague of Uto asserts that the greater the earnings retention ratio, the greater the sustainable growth rate because g is a positive function of b. The colleague argues that Brother should decrease payout ratio. Explain the flaw in that argument.

14. An analyst following Chevron Corp. (NYSE Euronext: CVX) wants to estimate the sustainable growth rate for the company by using the PRAT model. For this purpose, the analyst has compiled the data in the following table. Assets and equity values are for the end of the year; the analyst uses averages of beginning and ending balance sheet values in computing ratios based on total assets and shareholders' equity. For example, average total assets for 2007 would be computed as $(148,786 + 132,628)/2 = \$140,707$. *Note*: All numbers except for EPS and DPS are in \$ millions.

Item	2007	2006	2005	2004
Net income	$18,688	$17,138	$14,099	$13,328
Sales	214,091	204,892	193,641	150,865
Total assets	148,786	132,628	125,833	93,208
Shareholders' quity	77,088	68,935	62,676	45,230
EPS	8.77	7.80	6.54	6.28
DPS	2.26	2.01	1.75	1.53

Source: Financial statements from Chevron's web site.

A. Compute the average value of each PRAT component during 2005–2007.
B. Using the overall mean value of the average component values calculated in part A, estimate the sustainable growth rate for Chevron.
C. Judge whether Chevron has reached a mature growth stage.

15. Casey Hyunh is trying to value the stock of Resources Limited. To easily see how a change in one or more of her assumptions affects the estimated value of the stock, she is using a spreadsheet model. The model has projections for the next four years based on the following assumptions.
   • Sales will be $300 million in year 1.
   • Sales will grow at 15 percent in years 2 and 3 and at 10 percent in year 4.
   • Operating profits (EBIT) will be 17 percent of sales in each year.
   • Interest expense will be $10 million per year.
   • Income tax rate is 30 percent.
   • Earnings retention ratio would stay at 0.60.
   • The per-share dividend growth rate will be constant from year 4 forward and this final growth rate will be 200 basis points less than the growth rate from year 3 to year 4.

   The company has 10 million shares outstanding. Hyunh has estimated the required return on Resources' stock to be 13 percent.
   A. Estimate the value of the stock at the end of year 4 based on the preceding assumptions.
   B. Estimate the current value of the stock using the same assumptions.
   C. Hyunh is wondering how a change in the projected sales growth rate would affect the estimated value. Estimate the current value of the stock if the sales growth rate in year 3 is 10 percent instead of 15 percent.

The following information relates to Questions 16 through 21.

Jacob Daniel is the chief investment officer at a U.S. pension fund sponsor and Steven Rae is an analyst for the pension fund who follows consumer/noncyclical stocks. At the beginning of 2009, Daniel asks Rae to value the equity of Tasty Foods Company for its possible inclusion in the list of approved investments. Tasty Foods Company is involved in the production of frozen foods that are sold under its own brand name to retailers.

Rae is considering whether a dividend discount model would be appropriate for valuing Tasty Foods. He has compiled the information in the following table for the company's EPS and DPS during the past five years. The quarterly dividends paid by the company have been added to arrive at the annual dividends. Rae has also computed the dividend payout ratio for each year as DPS/EPS and the growth rates in EPS and DPS.

Year	EPS ($)	DPS ($)	Payout Ratio	Growth in EPS	Growth in DPS
2008	2.12	0.59	0.278	2.9%	3.5%
2007	2.06	0.57	0.277	2.5	5.6
2006	2.01	0.54	0.269	6.3	5.9
2005	1.89	0.51	0.270	6.2	6.3
2004	1.78	0.48	0.270		

Rae notes that the EPS of the company has been increasing at an average rate of 4.48 percent per year. The dividend payout ratio has remained fairly stable and dividends have increased at an average rate of 5.30 percent. In view of a history of dividend payments by the company and the understandable relationship dividend policy bears to the company's earnings, Rae concludes that the DDM is appropriate to value the equity of Tasty Foods. Further, he expects the moderate growth rate of the company to persist and decides to use the Gordon growth model.

Rae uses the CAPM to compute the return on equity. He uses the annual yield of 4 percent on the 10-year Treasury bond as the risk-free return. He estimates the expected U.S. equity risk premium, with the S&P 500 Index used as a proxy for the market, to be 6.5 percent per year. The estimated beta of Tasty Foods against the S&P 500 Index is 1.10. Accordingly, Rae's estimate for the required return on equity for Tasty Foods is 0.04 + 1.10(0.065) = 0.1115 or 11.15 percent.

Using the past growth rate in dividends of 5.30 percent as his estimate of the future growth rate in dividends, Rae computes the value of Tasty Foods stock. He shows his analysis to Alex Renteria, his colleague at the pension fund who specializes in the frozen foods industry. Renteria concurs with the valuation approach used by Rae but disagrees with the future growth rate he used. Renteria believes that the stock's current price of $8.42 is the fair value of the stock.

16. Which of the following is closest to Rae's estimate of the stock's value?
    A. $10.08
    B. $10.54
    C. $10.62

17. What is the stock's justified trailing P/E based on the stock's value estimated by Rae?
    A. 5.01
    B. 5.24
    C. 5.27

18. Rae considers a security trading within a band of ±10 percent of his estimate of intrinsic value to be within a fair value range. By that criterion, the stock of Tasty Foods is
    A. Undervalued.
    B. Fairly valued.
    C. Overvalued.

19. The beta of Tasty Foods stock of 1.10 used by Rae in computing the required return on equity was based on monthly returns for the past 10 years. If Rae uses daily returns for the past 5 years, the beta estimate is 1.25. If a beta of 1.25 is used, what would be Rae's estimate of the value of the stock of Tasty Foods?
    A. $8.64
    B. $9.10
    C. $20.13

20. Alex Renteria has suggested that the market price of Tasty Foods stock is its fair value. What is the implied growth rate of dividends given the stock's market price? Use the required return on equity based on a beta of 1.10.
   A. 3.87%
   B. 5.30%
   C. 12.1%

21. If Alex Renteria is correct that the current price of Tasty Foods stock is its fair value, what is expected capital gains yield on the stock?
   A. 3.87%
   B. 4.25%
   C. 5.30%

The following information relates to Questions 22 through 27.

Assorted Fund, a UK-based globally diversified equity mutual fund, is considering adding Talisman Energy Inc. (Toronto Stock Exchange: TLM) to its portfolio. Talisman is an independent upstream oil and gas company headquartered in Calgary, Canada. It is one of the largest oil and gas companies in Canada and has operations in several countries. Brian Dobson, an analyst at the mutual fund, has been assigned the task of estimating a fair value of Talisman. Dobson is aware of several approaches that could be used for this purpose. After carefully considering the characteristics of the company and its competitors, he believes the company will have extraordinary growth for the next few years and normal growth thereafter. He has therefore concluded that a two-stage DDM is the most appropriate for valuing the stock.

Talisman pays semiannual dividends. The total dividends during 2006, 2007, and 2008 have been C$0.114, C$0.15, and C$0.175, respectively. These imply a growth rate of 32 percent in 2007 and 17 percent in 2008. Dobson believes that the growth rate will be 14 percent in the next year. He has estimated that the first stage will include the next eight years.

Dobson is using the CAPM to estimate the required return on equity for Talisman. He has estimated that the beta of Talisman, as measured against the S&P/TSX Composite Index (formerly TSE 300 Composite Index), is 0.84. The Canadian risk-free rate, as measured by the annual yield on the 10-year government bond, is 4.1 percent. The equity risk premium for the Canadian market is estimated at 5.5 percent. Based on these data, Dobson has estimated that the required return on Talisman stock is $0.041 + 0.84(0.055) = 0.0872$ or 8.72 percent. Dobson is doing the analysis in January 2008 and the stock price at that time is C$17.

Dobson realizes that even within the two-stage DDM, there could be some variations in the approach. He would like to explore how these variations affect the valuation of the stock. Specifically, he wants to estimate the value of the stock for each of the following approaches separately.

   I. The dividend growth rate will be 14 percent throughout the first stage of eight years. The dividend growth rate thereafter will be 7 percent.
   II. Instead of using the estimated stable growth rate of 7 percent in the second stage, Dobson wants to use his estimate that eight years later Talisman's stock will be worth 17 times its earnings per share (trailing P/E of 17). He expects that the earnings retention ratio at that time will be 0.70.
   III. In contrast to the first approach in which the growth rate declines abruptly from 14 percent in the eighth year to 7 percent in the ninth, the growth rate would decline linearly from 14 percent in the first year to 7 percent in the ninth.

22. What is the terminal value of the stock based on the first approach?
    A. C$17.65
    B. C$31.06
    C. C$33.09

23. In the first approach, what proportion of the total value of the stock is represented by the value of the second stage?
    A. 0.10
    B. 0.52
    C. 0.90

24. What is the terminal value of the stock based on the second approach (earnings multiple)?
    A. C$12.12
    B. C$28.29
    C. C$33.09

25. What is the current value of the stock based on the second approach?
    A. C$16.24
    B. C$17.65
    C. C$28.29

26. Based on the third approach (the H-model), the stock is
    A. Undervalued.
    B. Fairly valued.
    C. Overvalued.

27. Dobson is wondering what the consequences would be if the duration of the first stage was assumed to be 11 years instead of 8, with all the other assumptions/estimates remaining the same. Considering this change, which of the following is true?
    A. In the second approach, the proportion of the total value of the stock represented by the second stage would not change.
    B. The total value estimated using the third approach would increase.
    C. Using this new assumption and the first approach will lead Dobson to conclude that the stock is overvalued.

CHAPTER 4

FREE CASH FLOW VALUATION

LEARNING OUTCOMES

After completing this chapter, you will be able to do the following:

- Define and interpret free cash flow to the firm (FCFF) and free cash flow to equity (FCFE).
- Describe, compare, and contrast the FCFF and FCFE approaches to valuation.
- Contrast the ownership perspective implicit in the FCFE approach to the ownership perspective implicit in the dividend discount approach.
- Discuss the appropriate adjustments to net income, earnings before interest and taxes (EBIT), earnings before interest, taxes, depreciation, and amortization (EBITDA), and cash flow from operations (CFO) to calculate FCFF and FCFE.
- Calculate FCFF and FCFE when given a company's financial statements prepared according to International Financial Reporting Standards (IFRS) or U.S. generally accepted accounting principles (GAAP).
- Discuss approaches for forecasting FCFF and FCFE.
- Contrast the recognition of value in the FCFE model to the recognition of value in dividend discount models.
- Explain how dividends, share repurchases, share issues, and changes in leverage may affect FCFF and FCFE.
- Critique the use of net income and EBITDA as proxies for cash flow in valuation.
- Discuss the single-stage (stable-growth), two-stage, and three-stage FCFF and FCFE models (including assumptions) and explain the company characteristics that would justify the use of each model.
- Calculate the value of a company by using the stable-growth, two-stage, and three-stage FCFF and FCFE models.
- Explain how sensitivity analysis can be used in FCFF and FCFE valuations.
- Discuss approaches for calculating the terminal value in a multistage valuation model.
- Describe the characteristics of companies for which the FCFF model is preferred to the FCFE model.

SUMMARY OVERVIEW

Discounted cash flow models are widely used by analysts to value companies.

- Free cash flow to the firm (FCFF) and free cash flow to equity (FCFE) are the cash flows available to, respectively, all of the investors in the company and to common stockholders.
- Analysts like to use free cash flow (either FCFF or FCFE) as the return
  - If the company is not paying dividends.
  - If the company pays dividends but the dividends paid differ significantly from the company's capacity to pay dividends.
  - If free cash flows align with profitability within a reasonable forecast period with which the analyst is comfortable.
  - If the investor takes a control perspective.
- The FCFF valuation approach estimates the value of the firm as the present value of future FCFF discounted at the weighted average cost of capital:

$$\text{Firm value} = \sum_{t=1}^{\infty} \frac{\text{FCFF}_t}{(1 + \text{WACC})^t}$$

The value of equity is the value of the firm minus the value of the firm's debt:

$$\text{Equity value} = \text{Firm value} - \text{Market value of debt}$$

Dividing the total value of equity by the number of outstanding shares gives the value per share.

The WACC formula is

$$\text{WACC} = \frac{\text{MV(Debt)}}{\text{MV(Debt)} + \text{MV(Equity)}} r_d (1 - \text{Tax rate}) + \frac{\text{MV(Equity)}}{\text{MV(Debt)} + \text{MV(Equity)}} r$$

- The value of the firm if FCFF is growing at a constant rate is

$$\text{Firm value} = \frac{\text{FCFF}_1}{\text{WACC} - g} = \frac{\text{FCFF}_0(1 + g)}{\text{WACC} - g}$$

- With the FCFE valuation approach, the value of equity can be found by discounting FCFE at the required rate of return on equity, r:

$$\text{Equity value} = \sum_{t=1}^{\infty} \frac{\text{FCFE}_t}{(1 + r)^t}$$

Dividing the total value of equity by the number of outstanding shares gives the value per share.

- The value of equity if FCFE is growing at a constant rate is

$$\text{Equity value} = \frac{\text{FCFE}_1}{r - g} = \frac{\text{FCFE}_0(1 + g)}{r - g}$$

- FCFF and FCFE are frequently calculated by starting with net income:

$$\text{FCFF} = \text{NI} + \text{NCC} + \text{Int}(1-\text{Tax rate}) - \text{FCInv} - \text{WCInv}$$
$$\text{FCFE} = \text{NI} + \text{NCC} - \text{FCInv} - \text{WCInv} + \text{Net borrowing}$$

- FCFF and FCFE are related to each other as follows:

$$\text{FCFE} = \text{FCFF} - \text{Int}(1 - \text{Tax rate}) + \text{Net borrowing}$$

- FCFF and FCFE can be calculated by starting from cash flow from operations:

$$\text{FCFF} = \text{CFO} + \text{Int}(1 - \text{Tax rate}) - \text{FCInv}$$
$$\text{FCFE} = \text{CFO} - \text{FCInv} + \text{Net borrowing}$$

- FCFF can also be calculated from EBIT or EBITDA:

$$\text{FCFF} = \text{EBIT}(1 - \text{Tax rate}) + \text{Dep} - \text{FCInv} - \text{WCInv}$$
$$\text{FCFF} = \text{EBITDA}(1 - \text{Tax rate}) + \text{Dep}(\text{Tax rate}) - \text{FCInv} - \text{WCInv}$$

  FCFE can then be found by using $\text{FCFE} = \text{FCFF} - \text{Int}(1 - \text{Tax rate}) + \text{Net borrowing}$.
- Finding CFO, FCFF, and FCFE may require careful interpretation of corporate financial statements. In some cases, the needed information may not be transparent.
- Earnings components such as net income, EBIT, EBITDA, and CFO should not be used as cash flow measures to value a firm. These earnings components either double-count or ignore parts of the cash flow stream.
- FCFF or FCFE valuation expressions can be easily adapted to accommodate complicated capital structures, such as those that include preferred stock.
- A general expression for the two-stage FCFF valuation model is

$$\text{Firm value} = \sum_{t=1}^{n} \frac{\text{FCFF}_t}{(1 + \text{WACC})^t} + \frac{\text{FCFF}_{n+1}}{(\text{WACC} - g)} \frac{1}{(1 + \text{WACC})^n}$$

- A general expression for the two-stage FCFE valuation model is

$$\text{Equity value} = \sum_{t=1}^{n} \frac{\text{FCFE}_t}{(1 + r)^t} + \frac{\text{FCFE}_{n+1}}{r - g} \frac{1}{(1 + r)^n}$$

- One common two-stage model assumes a constant growth rate in each stage, and a second common model assumes declining growth in stage 1 followed by a long-run sustainable growth rate in stage 2.
- To forecast FCFF and FCFE, analysts build a variety of models of varying complexity. A common approach is to forecast sales, with profitability, investments, and financing derived from changes in sales.
- Three-stage models are often considered to be good approximations for cash flow streams that, in reality, fluctuate from year to year.
- Nonoperating assets, such as excess cash and marketable securities, noncurrent investment securities, and nonperforming assets, are usually segregated from the company's operating assets. They are valued separately and then added to the value of the company's operating assets to find total firm value.

PROBLEMS

1. Indicate the effect on this period's FCFF and FCFE of a change in each of the items listed here. Assume a $100 increase in each case and a 40 percent tax rate.
   A. Net income.
   B. Cash operating expenses.
   C. Depreciation.
   D. Interest expense.
   E. EBIT.
   F. Accounts receivable.
   G. Accounts payable.
   H. Property, plant, and equipment.
   I. Notes payable.
   J. Cash dividends paid.
   K. Proceeds from issuing new common shares.
   L. Common shares repurchased.

2. LaForge Systems, Inc. has net income of $285 million for the year 2008. Using information from the company's financial statements given here, show the adjustments to net income that would be required to find:
   A. FCFF.
   B. FCFE.
   C. In addition, show the adjustments to FCFF that would result in FCFE.

LaForge Systems, Inc., Balance Sheet

In millions	31 December 2007	2008
Assets		
Current assets		
Cash and equivalents	$ 210	$ 248
Accounts receivable	474	513
Inventory	520	564
Total current assets	1,204	1,325
Gross fixed assets	2,501	2,850
Accumulated depreciation	(604)	(784)
Net fixed assets	1,897	2,066
Total assets	$3,101	$3,391
Liabilities and shareholders' equity		
Current liabilities		
Accounts payable	$ 295	$ 317
Notes payable	300	310
Accrued taxes and expenses	76	99
Total current liabilities	671	726

In millions	31 December 2007	2008
Long-term debt	1,010	1,050
Common stock	50	50
Additional paid-in capital	300	300
Retained earnings	1,070	1,265
Total shareholders' equity	1,420	1,615
Total liabilities and shareholders' equity	$3,101	$3,391

Statement of Income

In millions, except per-share data	31 December 2008
Total revenues	$2,215
Operating costs and expenses	1,430
EBITDA	785
Depreciation	180
EBIT	605
Interest expense	130
Income before tax	475
Taxes (at 40 percent)	190
Net income	285
Dividends	90
Addition to retained earnings	195

Statement of Cash Flows

In millions	13 December 2008
Operating activities	
Net income	$ 285
Adjustments	
Depreciation	180
Changes in working capital	
Accounts receivable	(39)
Inventories	(44)
Accounts payable	22
Accrued taxes and expenses	23
Cash provided by operating activities	$427
Investing activities	
Purchases of fixed assets	349
Cash used for investing activities	$349

(*Continued*)

In millions	13 December 2008
Financing activities	
Notes payable	(10)
Long-term financing issuances	(40)
Common stock dividends	90
Cash used for financing activities	$40
Cash and equivalents increase (decrease)	38
Cash and equivalents at beginning of year	210
Cash and equivalents at end of year	$248
Supplemental cash flow disclosures	
Interest paid	$130
Income taxes paid	$190

Note: The Statement of Cash Flows shows the use of a convention by which the positive numbers of $349 and $40 for cash used for investing activities and cash used for financing activities, respectively, are understood to be subtractions, because "cash used" is an outflow.

3. For LaForge Systems, whose financial statements are given in problem 2, show the adjustments from the current levels of CFO (which is $427 million), EBIT ($605 million), and EBITDA ($785 million) to find
   A. FCFF.
   B. FCFE.

4. The term *free cash flow* is frequently applied to cash flows that differ from the definition for FCFF that should be used to value a firm. Two such definitions of free cash flow are given below. Compare these two definitions for free cash flow with the technically correct definition of FCFF used in the text.
   A. FCF = Net income + Depreciation and amortization − Cash dividends − Capital expenditures.
   B. FCF = Cash flow from operations (from the statement of cash flows) − Capital expenditures.

5. Proust Company has FCFF of $1.7 billion and FCFE of $1.3 billion. Proust's WACC is 11 percent, and its required rate of return for equity is 13 percent. FCFF is expected to grow forever at 7 percent, and FCFE is expected to grow forever at 7.5 percent. Proust has debt outstanding of $15 billion.
   A. What is the total value of Proust's equity using the FCFF valuation approach?
   B. What is the total value of Proust's equity using the FCFE valuation approach?

6. Quinton Johnston is evaluating TMI Manufacturing Company, Ltd., which is headquartered in Taiwan. In 2008, when Johnston is performing his analysis, the company is unprofitable. Furthermore, TMI pays no dividends on its common shares. Johnston decides to value TMI Manufacturing by using his forecasts of FCFE. Johnston gathers the following facts and assumptions:
   • The company has 17.0 billion shares outstanding.
   • Sales will be $5.5 billion in 2009, increasing at 28 percent annually for the next four years (through 2013).

- Net income will be 32 percent of sales.
- Investment in fixed assets will be 35 percent of sales; investment in working capital will be 6 percent of sales; depreciation will be 9 percent of sales.
- 20 percent of the investment in assets will be financed with debt.
- Interest expenses will be only 2 percent of sales.
- The tax rate will be 10 percent. TMI Manufacturing's beta is 2.1; the risk-free government bond rate is 6.4 percent; the equity risk premium is 5.0 percent.
- At the end of 2013, Johnston projects TMI will sell for 18 times earnings.

What is the value of one ordinary share of TMI Manufacturing Company?

7. Do Pham is evaluating Phaneuf Accelerateur by using the FCFF and FCFE valuation approaches. Pham has collected the following information (currency in euro):
   - Phaneuf has net income of €250 million, depreciation of €90 million, capital expenditures of €170 million, and an increase in working capital of €40 million.
   - Phaneuf will finance 40 percent of the increase in net fixed assets (capital expenditures less depreciation) and 40 percent of the increase in working capital with debt financing.
   - Interest expenses are €150 million. The current market value of Phaneuf's outstanding debt is €1,800 million.
   - FCFF is expected to grow at 6.0 percent indefinitely, and FCFE is expected to grow at 7.0 percent.
   - The tax rate is 30 percent.
   - Phaneuf is financed with 40 percent debt and 60 percent equity. The before-tax cost of debt is 9 percent, and the before-tax cost of equity is 13 percent.
   - Phaneuf has 10 million outstanding shares.
   A. Using the FCFF valuation approach, estimate the total value of the firm, the total market value of equity, and the per-share value of equity.
   B. Using the FCFE valuation approach, estimate the total market value of equity and the per-share value of equity.

8. PHB Company currently sells for $32.50 per share. In an attempt to determine whether PHB is fairly priced, an analyst has assembled the following information:
   - The before-tax required rates of return on PHB debt, preferred stock, and common stock are, respectively, 7.0 percent, 6.8 percent, and 11.0 percent.
   - The company's target capital structure is 30 percent debt, 15 percent preferred stock, and 55 percent common stock.
   - The market value of the company's debt is $145 million, and its preferred stock is valued at $65 million.
   - PHB's FCFF for the year just ended is $28 million. FCFF is expected to grow at a constant rate of 4 percent for the foreseeable future.
   - The tax rate is 35 percent.
   - PHB has 8 million outstanding common shares.

What is PHB's estimated value per share? Is PHB's stock underpriced?

9. Watson Dunn is planning to value BCC Corporation, a provider of a variety of industrial metals and minerals. Dunn uses a single-stage FCFF approach. The financial information Dunn has assembled for his valuation is as follows:
   - The company has 1,852 million shares outstanding.
   - The market value of its debt is $3.192 billion.

- The FCFF is currently $1.1559 billion.
- The equity beta is 0.90; the equity risk premium is 5.5 percent; the risk-free rate is 5.5 percent.
- The before-tax cost of debt is 7.0 percent.
- The tax rate is 40 percent.
- To calculate WACC, he will assume the company is financed 25 percent with debt.
- The FCFF growth rate is 4 percent.

Using Dunn's information, calculate the following:
A. WACC.
B. Value of the firm.
C. Total market value of equity.
D. Value per share.

10. Kenneth McCoin is valuing McInish Corporation and performing a sensitivity analysis on his valuation. He uses a single-stage FCFE growth model. The base-case values for each of the parameters in the model are given, together with possible low and high estimates for each variable, in the following table.

Variable	Base-Case Value	Low Estimate	High Estimate
Normalized $FCFE_0$	$0.88	$0.70	$1.14
Risk-free rate	5.08%	5.00%	5.20%
Equity risk premium	5.50%	4.50%	6.50%
Beta	0.70	0.60	0.80
FCFE growth rate	6.40%	4.00%	7.00%

A. Use the base-case values to estimate the current value of McInish Corporation.
B. Calculate the range of stock prices that would occur if the base-case value for $FCFE_0$ were replaced by the low estimate and the high estimate for $FCFE_0$. Similarly, using the base-case values for all other variables, calculate the range of stock prices caused by using the low and high values for beta, the risk-free rate, the equity risk premium, and the growth rate. Based on these ranges, rank the sensitivity of the stock price to each of the five variables.

11. An aggressive financial planner who claims to have a superior method for picking undervalued stocks is courting one of your clients. The planner claims that the best way to find the value of a stock is to divide EBITDA by the risk-free bond rate. The planner is urging your client to invest in NewMarket, Inc. The planner says that NewMarket's EBITDA of $1,580 million divided by the long-term government bond rate of 7 percent gives a total value of $22,571.4 million. With 318 million outstanding shares, NewMarket's value per share found by using this method is $70.98. Shares of NewMarket currently trade for $36.50.
A. Provide your client with an alternative estimate of NewMarket's value per share based on a two-stage FCFE valuation approach. Use the following assumptions:
   - Net income is currently $600 million. Net income will grow by 20 percent annually for the next three years.
   - The net investment in operating assets (capital expenditures less depreciation plus investment in working capital) will be $1,150 million next year and grow at 15 percent for the following two years.

- Forty percent of the net investment in operating assets will be financed with net new debt financing.
- NewMarket's beta is 1.3; the risk-free bond rate is 7 percent; the equity risk premium is 4 percent.
- After three years, the growth rate of net income will be 8 percent and the net investment in operating assets (capital expenditures minus depreciation plus increase in working capital) each year will drop to 30 percent of net income.
- Debt is, and will continue to be, 40 percent of total assets.
- NewMarket has 318 million shares outstanding.

B. Criticize the valuation approach that the aggressive financial planner used.

12. Bron has EPS of $3.00 in 2002 and expects EPS to increase by 21 percent in 2003. Earnings per share are expected to grow at a decreasing rate for the following five years, as shown in the following table.

	2003	2004	2005	2006	2007	2008
Growth rate for EPS	21%	18%	15%	12%	9%	6%
Net capital expenditures per share	$5.00	$5.00	$4.50	$4.00	$3.50	$1.50

In 2008, the growth rate will be 6 percent and is expected to stay at that rate thereafter. Net capital expenditures (capital expenditures minus depreciation) will be $5.00 per share in 2002 and then follow the pattern predicted in the table. In 2008, net capital expenditures are expected to be $1.50 and will then grow at 6 percent annually. The investment in working capital parallels the increase in net capital expenditures and is predicted to equal 25 percent of net capital expenditures each year. In 2008, investment in working capital will be $0.375 and is predicted to grow at 6 percent thereafter. Bron will use debt financing to fund 40 percent of net capital expenditures and 40 percent of the investment in working capital. The required rate of return for Bron is 12 percent.

Estimate the value of a Bron share using a two-stage FCFE valuation approach.

13. The management of Telluride, an international diversified conglomerate based in the United States, believes that the recent strong performance of its wholly owned medical supply subsidiary, Sundanci, has gone unnoticed. To realize Sundanci's full value, Telluride has announced that it will divest Sundanci in a tax-free spin-off.

Sue Carroll, CFA, is director of research at Kesson and Associates. In developing an investment recommendation for Sundanci, Carroll has gathered the information shown in Exhibits 4-1 and 4-2.

EXHIBIT 4-1   Sundanci Actual 2007 and 2008 Financial Statements for Fiscal Years Ending 31 May (dollars in millions except per-share data)

Income Statement	2007	2008
Revenue	$474	$598
Depreciation	20	23
Other operating costs	368	460
Income before taxes	86	115
Taxes	26	35

(Continued)

EXHIBIT 4-1   (*Continued*)

Income Statement	2007	2008
Net income	60	80
Dividends	18	24
EPS	$0.714	$0.952
Dividends per share	$0.214	$0.286
Common shares outstanding	84.0	84.0
Balance Sheet		
Current assets (includes $5 cash in 2007 and 2008)	$201	$326
Net property, plant, and equipment	474	489
Total assets	675	815
Current liabilities (all non-interest-bearing)	57	141
Long-term debt	0	0
Total liabilities		
Shareholders' equity	618	674
Total liabilities and equity	675	815
Capital expenditures	34	38

EXHIBIT 4-2   Selected Financial Information

Required rate of return on equity	14%
Industry growth rate	13%
Industry P/E	26

Abbey Naylor, CFA, has been directed by Carroll to determine the value of Sundanci's stock by using the FCFE model. Naylor believes that Sundanci's FCFE will grow at 27 percent for two years and at 13 percent thereafter. Capital expenditures, depreciation, and working capital are all expected to increase proportionately with FCFE.
A. Calculate the amount of FCFE per share for 2008 by using the data from Exhibit 4-1.
B. Calculate the current value of a share of Sundanci stock based on the two-stage FCFE model.
C. Describe limitations that the two-stage DDM and FCFE models have in common.

14. John Jones, CFA, is head of the research department of Peninsular Research. One of the companies he is researching, Mackinac Inc., is a U.S.-based manufacturing company. Mackinac has released the June 2007 financial statements shown in Exhibits 4-3, 4-4, and 4-5.

EXHIBIT 4-3   Mackinac Inc. Annual Income Statement
30 June 2007 (in thousands, except per-share data)

Sales	$250,000
Cost of goods sold	125,000
Gross operating profit	125,000

(*Continued*)

EXHIBIT 4-3   (*Continued*)

Selling, general, and administrative expenses	50,000
EBITDA	75,000
Depreciation and amortization	10,500
EBIT	64,500
Interest expense	11,000
Pretax income	53,500
Income taxes	16,050
Net income	$37,450
Shares outstanding	13,000
EPS	$2.88

EXHIBIT 4-4   Mackinac Inc. Balance Sheet 30 June 2007 (in thousands)

Current Assets		
Cash and equivalents	$20,000	
Receivables	40,000	
Inventories	29,000	
Other current assets	23,000	
Total current assets		$112,000
Noncurrent Assets		
Property, plant, and equipment	$145,000	
Less: Accumulated depreciation	43,000	
Net property, plant, and equipment	102,000	
Investments	70,000	
Other noncurrent assets	36,000	
Total noncurrent assets		208,000
Total assets		$320,000
Current Liabilities		
Accounts payable	$41,000	
Short-term debt	12,000	
Other current liabilities	17,000	
Total current liabilities		$70,000
Noncurrent Liabilities		
Long-term debt	100,000	
Total noncurrent liabilities		100,000
Total liabilities		170,000
Shareholders' Equity		
Common equity	40,000	
Retained earnings	110,000	
Total equity		150,000
Total liabilities and equity		$320,000

EXHIBIT 4-5   Mackinac Inc. Cash Flow Statement 30 June 2007
(in thousands)

Cash Flow from Operating Activities		
Net income		$37,450
Depreciation and amortization		10,500
Change in Working Capital		
(Increase) decrease in receivables	($5,000)	
(Increase) decrease in inventories	(8,000)	
Increase (decrease) in payables	6,000	
Increase (decrease) in other current liabilities	1,500	
Net change in working capital		(5,500)
Net cash from operating activities		$42,450
Cash Flow from Investing Activities		
Purchase of property, plant, and equipment	($15,000)	
Net cash from investing activities		($15,000)
Cash Flow from Financing Activities		
Change in debt outstanding	$4,000	
Payment of cash dividends	(22,470)	
Net cash from financing activities		(18,470)
Net change in cash and cash equivalents		$8,980
Cash at beginning of period		11,020
Cash at end of period		$20,000

Mackinac has announced that it has finalized an agreement to handle North American production of a successful product currently marketed by a company headquartered outside North America. Jones decides to value Mackinac by using the DDM and FCFE models. After reviewing Mackinac's financial statements and forecasts related to the new production agreement, Jones concludes the following:
- Mackinac's earnings and FCFE are expected to grow 17 percent a year over the next three years before stabilizing at an annual growth rate of 9 percent.
- Mackinac will maintain the current payout ratio.
- Mackinac's beta is 1.25.
- The government bond yield is 6 percent, and the market equity risk premium is 5 percent.
A. Calculate the value of a share of Mackinac's common stock by using the two-stage DDM.
B. Calculate the value of a share of Mackinac's common stock by using the two-stage FCFE model.
C. Jones is discussing with a corporate client the possibility of that client acquiring a 70 percent interest in Mackinac. Discuss whether the DDM or FCFE model is more appropriate for this client's valuation purposes.

15. SK Telecom Company is a cellular telephone paging and computer communication services company in Seoul, South Korea. The company is traded on the Korea, New York, and London stock exchanges (NYSE: SKM). Sol Kim has estimated the normalized FCFE for SK Telecom to be 1,300 Korean won (per share) for the year just ended. The real country return for South Korea is 6.50 percent. To estimate the required return for SK Telecom, Kim makes the following adjustments to the real country return: an industry adjustment of +0.60 percent, a size adjustment of −0.10 percent, and a leverage adjustment of +0.25 percent. The long-term real growth rate for South Korea is estimated to be 3.5 percent, and Kim expects the real growth rate of SK Telecom to track the country rate.
    A. What is the real required rate of return for SK Telecom?
    B. Using the single-stage FCFE valuation model and real values for the discount rate and FCFE growth rate, estimate the value of one share of SK Telecom.

16. Lawrence McKibben is preparing a valuation of QuickChange Auto Centers, Inc. McKibben has decided to use a three-stage FCFE valuation model and the following estimates. The FCFE per share for the current year is $0.75. The FCFE is expected to grow at 10 percent for next year, then at 26 percent annually for the following three years, and then at 6 percent in year 5 and thereafter. QuickChange's estimated beta is 2.00, and McKibben believes that current market conditions dictate a 4.5 percent risk-free rate of return and a 5.0 percent equity risk premium. Given McKibben's assumptions and approach, estimate the value of a share of QuickChange.

17. Clay Cooperman has valued the operating assets of Johnson Extrusion at $720 million. The company also has short-term cash and securities with a market value of $60 million that are not needed for Johnson's operations. The noncurrent investments have a book value of $30 million and a market value of $45 million. The company also has an overfunded pension plan, with plan assets of $210 million and plan liabilities of $170 million. Johnson Extrusion has $215 million of notes and bonds outstanding and 100 million outstanding shares. What is the value per share of Johnson Extrusion stock?

Use the following information to answer Questions 18 through 23.

Ryan Leigh is preparing a presentation that analyzes the valuation of the common stock of two companies under consideration as additions to his firm's recommended list, Emerald Corporation and Holt Corporation. Leigh has prepared preliminary valuations of both companies using an FCFE model and is also preparing a value estimate for Emerald using a dividend discount model. Holt's 2007 and 2008 financial statements, contained in Exhibits 4-6 and 4-7, are prepared in accordance with U.S. GAAP.

EXHIBIT 4-6   Holt Corporation Consolidated Balance Sheets
(US$ millions)

	As of 31 December	
	2008	2007
Assets		
Current assets		
Cash and cash equivalents	$372	$315
Accounts receivable	770	711
		(Continued)

EXHIBIT 4-6   (*Continued*)

	As of 31 December			
		2008		2007
Inventories		846		780
Total current assets		1,988		1,806
Gross fixed assets	4,275		3,752	
Less: Accumulated depreciation	1,176	3,099	906	2,846
Total assets		$5,087		$4,652
Liabilities and shareholders' equity				
Current liabilities				
Accounts payable		$476		$443
Accrued taxes and expenses		149		114
Notes payable		465		450
Total current liabilities		1,090		1,007
Long-term debt		1,575		1,515
Common stock		525		525
Retained earnings		1,897		1,605
Total liabilities and shareholders' equity		$5,087		$4,652

EXHIBIT 4-7   Holt Corporation Consolidated Income Statement for the Year Ended 31 December 2008 (US$ millions)

Total revenues	$ 3,323
Cost of goods sold	1,287
Selling, general, and administrative expenses	858
Earnings before interest, taxes, depreciation, and amortization (EBITDA)	1,178
Depreciation expense	270
Operating income	908
Interest expense	195
Pretax income	713
Income tax (at 32 percent)	228
Net income	$ 485

Leigh presents his valuations of the common stock of Emerald and Holt to his supervisor, Alice Smith. Smith has the following questions and comments:

- "I estimate that Emerald's long-term expected dividend payout rate is 20 percent and its return on equity is 10 percent over the long-term."
- "Why did you use an FCFE model to value Holt's common stock? Can you use a DDM instead?"

- "How did Holt's FCFE for 2008 compare with its FCFF for the same year? I recommend you use an FCFF model to value Holt's common stock instead of using an FCFE model because Holt has had a history of leverage changes in the past."
- "In the past three years, about 5 percent of Holt's growth in FCFE has come from decreases in inventory."

Leigh responds to each of Smith's points as follows:

- "I will use your estimates and calculate Emerald's long-term, sustainable dividend growth rate."
- "There are two reasons why I used the FCFE model to value Holt's common stock instead of using a DDM. The first reason is that Holt's dividends have differed significantly from its capacity to pay dividends. The second reason is that Holt is a takeover target and once the company is taken over, the new owners will have discretion over the uses of free cash flow."
- "I will calculate Holt's FCFF for 2008 and estimate the value of Holt's common stock using an FCFF model."
- "Holt is a growing company. In forecasting either Holt's FCFE or FCFF growth rates, I will not consider decreases in inventory to be a long-term source of growth."

18. Which of the following long-term FCFE growth rates is *most* consistent with the facts and stated policies of Emerald?
    A. 5 percent or lower.
    B. 2 percent or higher.
    C. 8 percent or higher.

19. Do the reasons provided by Leigh support his use of the FCFE model to value Holt's common stock instead of using a DDM?
    A. Yes.
    B. No, because Holt's dividend situation argues in favor of using the DDM.
    C. No, because FCFE is not appropriate for investors taking a control perspective.

20. Holt's FCFF (in millions) for 2008 is *closest* to:
    A. $308.
    B. $370.
    C. $422.

21. Holt's FCFE (in millions) for 2008 is *closest* to:
    A. $175.
    B. $250.
    C. $364.

22. Leigh's comment about not considering decreases in inventory to be a source of long-term growth in free cash flow for Holt is:
    A. Inconsistent with a forecasting perspective.
    B. Mistaken because decreases in inventory are a use rather than a source of cash.
    C. Consistent with a forecasting perspective because inventory reduction has a limit, particularly for a growing firm.

23. Smith's recommendation to use an FCFF model to value Holt is:
    A. Logical, given the prospect of Holt changing capital structure.
    B. Not logical because an FCFF model is used only to value the total firm.
    C. Not logical because FCFE represents a more direct approach to free cash flow valuation.

CHAPTER 5

RESIDUAL INCOME VALUATION

LEARNING OUTCOMES

After completing this chapter, you will be able to do the following:

- Calculate and interpret residual income and related measures (e.g., economic value added and market value added).
- Discuss the use of residual income models.
- Calculate future values of residual income given current book value, earnings growth estimates, and an assumed dividend payout ratio.
- Calculate the intrinsic value of a share of common stock using the residual income model.
- Discuss the fundamental determinants or drivers of residual income.
- Explain the relationship between residual income valuation and the justified price-to-book ratio based on forecasted fundamentals.
- Calculate and interpret the intrinsic value of a share of common stock using a single-stage (constant-growth) residual income model.
- Calculate an implied growth rate in residual income given the market price-to-book ratio and an estimate of the required rate of return on equity.
- Explain continuing residual income and list the common assumptions regarding continuing residual income.
- Justify an estimate of continuing residual income at the forecast horizon given company and industry prospects.
- Calculate and interpret the intrinsic value of a share of common stock using a multistage residual income model, given the required rate of return, forecasted earnings per share over a finite horizon, and forecasted continuing residual earnings.
- Explain the relationship of the residual income model to the dividend discount and free cash flow to equity models.
- Contrast the recognition of value in the residual income model to value recognition in other present value models.
- Discuss the strengths and weaknesses of the residual income model.
- Justify the selection of the residual income model for equity valuation, given characteristics of the company being valued.
- Discuss the major accounting issues in applying residual income models (e.g., clean surplus violations, variations from fair value, intangible asset effects on book value, and nonrecurring items) and appropriate analyst responses to each issue.

SUMMARY OVERVIEW

This chapter has discussed the use of residual income models in valuation. Residual income is an appealing economic concept because it attempts to measure economic profit, which is profit after accounting for all opportunity costs of capital.

- Residual income is calculated as net income minus a deduction for the cost of equity capital. The deduction is called the equity charge and is equal to equity capital multiplied by the required rate of return on equity (the cost of equity capital in percent).
- Economic value added (EVA) is a commercial implementation of the residual income concept.

$$EVA = NOPAT - (C\% \times TC)$$

where

$\quad$ NOPAT = net operating profit after taxes
$\quad\quad$ C% = the percent cost of capital
$\quad\quad$ TC = total capital.

- Residual income models (including commercial implementations) are used not only for equity valuation but also to measure internal corporate performance and for determining executive compensation.
- We can forecast per-share residual income as forecasted earnings per share minus the required rate of return on equity multiplied by beginning book value per share. Alternatively, per-share residual income can be forecasted as beginning book value per share multiplied by the difference between forecasted ROE and the required rate of return on equity.
- In the residual income model, the intrinsic value of a share of common stock is the sum of book value per share and the present value of expected future per-share residual income. In the residual income model, the equivalent mathematical expressions for intrinsic value of a common stock are

$$V_0 = B_0 + \sum_{t=1}^{\infty} \frac{RI_t}{(1+r)^t} = B_0 + \sum_{t=1}^{\infty} \frac{E_t - rB_{t-1}}{(1+r)^t} = B_0 + \sum_{t=1}^{\infty} \frac{(ROE_t - r)B_{t-1}}{(1+r)^t}$$

where

$\quad\quad V_0$ = value of a share of stock today ($t = 0$)
$\quad\quad B_0$ = current per-share book value of equity
$\quad\quad B_t$ = expected per-share book value of equity at any time t
$\quad\quad r$ = required rate of return on equity (cost of equity)
$\quad\quad E_t$ = expected earnings per share for period t
$\quad\quad RI_t$ = expected per-share residual income, equal to $E_t - rB_{t-1}$ or to $(ROE - r) \times B_{t-1}$

- In most cases, value is recognized earlier in the residual income model compared with other present value models of stock value, such as the dividend discount model.
- Strengths of the residual income model include the following:
  - Terminal values do not make up a large portion of the value relative to other models.
  - The model uses readily available accounting data.
  - The model can be used in the absence of dividends and near-term positive free cash flows.
  - The model can be used when cash flows are unpredictable.

- Weaknesses of the residual income model include the following:
  - The model is based on accounting data that can be subject to manipulation by management.
  - Accounting data used as inputs may require significant adjustments.
  - The model requires that the clean surplus relation holds, or that the analyst makes appropriate adjustments when the clean surplus relation does not hold.
- The residual income model is most appropriate in the following cases:
  - A company is not paying dividends or it exhibits an unpredictable dividend pattern.
  - A company has negative free cash flow many years out but is expected to generate positive cash flow at some point in the future.
  - A great deal of uncertainty exists in forecasting terminal values.
- The fundamental determinants or drivers of residual income are book value of equity and return on equity.
- Residual income valuation is most closely related to P/B. When the present value of expected future residual income is positive (negative), the justified P/B based on fundamentals is greater than (less than) one.
- When fully consistent assumptions are used to forecast earnings, cash flow, dividends, book value, and residual income through a full set of pro forma (projected) financial statements, and the same required rate of return on equity is used as the discount rate, the same estimate of value should result from a residual income, dividend discount, or free cash flow valuation. In practice, however, analysts may find one model easier to apply and possibly arrive at different valuations using the different models.
- Continuing residual income is residual income after the forecast horizon. Frequently, one of the following assumptions concerning continuing residual income is made:
  - Residual income continues indefinitely at a positive level. (One variation of this assumption is that residual income continues indefinitely at the rate of inflation, meaning it is constant in real terms.)
  - Residual income is zero from the terminal year forward.
  - Residual income declines to zero as ROE reverts to the cost of equity over time.
  - Residual income declines to some mean level.
- The residual income model assumes the clean surplus relation of $B_t = B_{t-1} + E_t - D_t$. In other terms, the ending book value of equity equals the beginning book value plus earnings minus dividends, apart from ownership transactions.
- In practice, to apply the residual income model most accurately, the analyst may need to
  - Adjust book value of common equity for
    - Off-balance-sheet items.
    - Discrepancies from fair value.
    - The amortization of certain intangible assets.
  - Adjust reported net income to reflect clean surplus accounting.
  - Adjust reported net income for nonrecurring items misclassified as recurring items.

PROBLEMS

1. Based on the following information, determine whether Vertically Integrated Manufacturing (VIM) earned any residual income for its shareholders:
   - VIM had total assets of $3,000,000, financed with twice as much debt capital as equity capital.

- VIM's pretax cost of debt is 6 percent and cost of equity capital is 10 percent.
- VIM had EBIT of $300,000 and was taxed at a rate of 40 percent.

Calculate residual income by using the method based on deducting an equity charge.

2. Use the following information to estimate the intrinsic value of VIM's common stock using the residual income model:
    - VIM had total assets of $3,000,000, financed with twice as much debt capital as equity capital.
    - VIM's pretax cost of debt is 6 percent and cost of equity capital is 10 percent.
    - VIM had EBIT of $300,000 and was taxed at a rate of 40 percent. EBIT is expected to continue at $300,000 indefinitely.
    - VIM's book value per share is $20.
    - VIM has 50,000 shares of common stock outstanding.

3. Palmetto Steel, Inc. (PSI) maintains a dividend payout ratio of 80 percent because of its limited opportunities for expansion. Its return on equity is 15 percent. The required rate of return on PSI equity is 12 percent, and its long-term growth rate is 3 percent. Compute the justified P/B based on forecasted fundamentals, consistent with the residual income model and a constant growth rate assumption.

4. Because New Market Products (NMP) markets consumer staples, it is able to make use of considerable debt in its capital structure; specifically, 90 percent of the company's total assets of $450,000,000 are financed with debt capital. Its cost of debt is 8 percent before taxes, and its cost of equity capital is 12 percent. NMP achieved a pretax income of $5.1 million in 2006 and had a tax rate of 40 percent. What was NMP's residual income?

5. In 2007, Smithson-Williams Investments (SWI) achieved an operating profit after taxes of €10 million on total assets of €100 million. Half of its assets were financed with debt with a pretax cost of 9 percent. Its cost of equity capital is 12 percent, and its tax rate is 40 percent. Did SWI achieve a positive residual income?

6. Calculate the economic value added (EVA) or residual income, as requested, for each of the following:
    A. NOPAT = $100
        Beginning book value of debt = $200
        Beginning book value of equity = $300
        WACC = 11 percent
        Calculate EVA.
    B. Net income = €5.00
        Dividends = €1.00
        Beginning book value of equity = €30.00
        Required rate of return on equity = 11 percent
        Calculate residual income.
    C. Return on equity = 18 percent
        Required rate of return on equity = 12 percent
        Beginning book value of equity = €30.00
        Calculate residual income.

7. Jim Martin is using economic value added (EVA) and market value added (MVA) to measure the performance of Sundanci. Martin uses the following fiscal year 2000 information for his analysis:

- Adjusted net operating profit after tax (NOPAT) is $100 million.
- Total capital is $700 million (no debt).
- Closing stock price is $26.
- Total shares outstanding is 84 million.
- The cost of equity is 14 percent.

Calculate the following for Sundanci. Show your work.
A. EVA for fiscal year 2000.
B. MVA as of fiscal year-end 2000.

8. Protected Steel Corporation (PSC) has a book value of $6 per share. PSC is expected to earn $0.60 per share forever and pays out all of its earnings as dividends. The required rate of return on PSC's equity is 12 percent. Calculate the value of the stock using the following:
   A. Dividend discount model.
   B. Residual income model.

9. Notable Books (NB) is a family controlled company that dominates the retail book market. NB has book value of $10 per share, is expected to earn $2.00 forever, and pays out all of its earnings as dividends. Its required return on equity is 12.5 percent. Value the stock of NB using the following:
   A. Dividend discount model.
   B. Residual income model.

10. Simonson Investment Trust International (SITI) is expected to earn $4.00, $5.00, and $8.00 for the next three years. SITI will pay annual dividends of $2.00, $2.50, and $20.50 in each of these years. The last dividend includes a liquidating payment to shareholders at the end of year 3 when the trust terminates. SITI's book value is $8 per share and its required return on equity is 10 percent.
    A. What is the current value per share of SITI according to the dividend discount model?
    B. Calculate per-share book value and residual income for SITI for each of the next three years and use those results to find the stock's value using the residual income model.
    C. Calculate return on equity and use it as an input to the residual income model to calculate SITI's value.

11. Foodsco Incorporated (FI), a leading distributor of food products and materials to restaurants and other institutions, has a remarkably steady track record in terms of both return on equity and growth. At year-end 2007, FI had a book value of $30 per share. For the foreseeable future, the company is expected to achieve an ROE of 15 percent (on trailing book value) and to pay out one-third of its earnings in dividends. The required return is 12 percent. Forecast FI's residual income for the year ending 31 December 2012.

12. Lendex Electronics (LE) had a great deal of turnover of top management for several years and was not followed by analysts during this period of turmoil. Because the company's performance has been improving steadily for the past three years, technology analyst Steve Kent recently reinitiated coverage of LE. A meeting with management confirmed Kent's positive impression of LE's operations and strategic plan. Kent decides LE merits further analysis.

Careful examination of LE's financial statements revealed that the company had negative other comprehensive income from changes in the value of available-for-sale securities in each of the past five years. How, if at all, should this observation about LE's other comprehensive income affect the figures that Kent uses for the company's ROE and book value for those years?

13. Retail fund manager Seymour Simms is considering the purchase of shares in upstart retailer Hot Topic Stores (HTS). The current book value of HTS is $20 per share, and its market price is $35. Simms expects long-term ROE to be 18 percent, long-term growth to be 10 percent, and cost of equity to be 14 percent. What conclusion would you expect Simms to arrive at if he uses a single-stage residual income model to value these shares?

14. Dayton Manufactured Homes (DMH) builds prefabricated homes and mobile homes. Favorable demographics and the likelihood of slow, steady increases in market share should enable DMH to maintain its ROE of 15 percent and growth rate of 10 percent through time. DMH has a book value of $30 per share and the required rate of return on its equity is 12 percent. Compute the value of its equity using the single-stage residual income model.

15. Use the following inputs and the finite horizon form of the residual income model to compute the value of Southern Trust Bank (STB) shares as of 31 December 2007:
    • ROE will continue at 15 percent for the next five years (and 10 percent thereafter) with all earnings reinvested (no dividends paid).
    • Cost of equity equals 10 percent.
    • B_0 = $10 per share (at year-end 2007).
    • Premium over book value at the end of five years will be 20 percent.

16. Shunichi Kobayashi is valuing United Parcel Service (NYSE: UPS). Kobayashi has made the following assumptions:
    • Book value per share is estimated at $9.62 on 31 December 2007.
    • EPS will be 22 percent of the beginning book value per share for the next eight years.
    • Cash dividends paid will be 30 percent of EPS.
    • At the end of the eight-year period, the market price per share will be three times the book value per share.
    • The beta for UPS is 0.60, the risk-free rate is 5.00 percent, and the equity risk premium is 5.50 percent.

    The current market price of UPS is $59.38, which indicates a current P/B of 6.2.
    A. Prepare a table that shows the beginning and ending book values, net income, and cash dividends annually for the eight-year period.
    B. Estimate the residual income and the present value of residual income for the eight years.
    C. Estimate the value per share of UPS stock using the residual income model.
    D. Estimate the value per share of UPS stock using the dividend discount model. How does this value compare with the estimate from the residual income model?

17. Boeing Company (NYSE: BA) has a current stock price of $49.86. It also has a P/B of 3.57 and book value per share of $13.97. Assume that the single-stage growth model is appropriate for valuing the company. Boeing's beta is 0.80, the risk-free rate is 5.00 percent, and the equity risk premium is 5.50 percent.
    A. If the growth rate is 6 percent and the ROE is 20 percent, what is the justified P/B for Boeing?
    B. If the growth rate is 6 percent, what ROE is required to yield Boeing's current P/B?
    C. If the ROE is 20 percent, what growth rate is required for Boeing to have its current P/B?

CHAPTER 6

MARKET-BASED VALUATION: PRICE AND ENTERPRISE VALUE MULTIPLES

LEARNING OUTCOMES

After completing this chapter, you will be able to do the following:

- Distinguish among types of valuation indicators.
- Distinguish between the method of comparables and the method based on forecasted fundamentals as approaches to using price multiples in valuation.
- Define a justified price multiple.
- Discuss the economic rationales for the method of comparables and the method based on forecasted fundamentals.
- List and discuss rationales for each price multiple and dividend yield in valuation.
- Discuss possible drawbacks to the use of each price multiple and dividend yield.
- Define and calculate each price multiple and dividend yield.
- Define underlying earnings and, given earnings per share (EPS) and nonrecurring items in the income statement, calculate underlying earnings.
- Define normalized EPS, discuss the methods of normalizing EPS, and calculate normalized EPS by each method.
- Explain and justify the use of earnings yield (i.e., EPS divided by share price).
- Identify and discuss the fundamental factors that influence each price multiple and dividend yield.
- Calculate the justified price-to-earnings ratio (P/E), price-to-book ratio, and price-to-sales ratio for a stock, based on forecasted fundamentals.
- Calculate a predicted P/E given a cross-sectional regression on fundamentals and explain limitations to the cross-sectional regression methodology.
- Define the benchmark value of a multiple.
- Evaluate a stock using the method of comparables.
- Discuss the importance of fundamentals in the method of comparables.
- Define and calculate the P/E-to-growth ratio and explain its use in relative valuation.

- Calculate and explain the use of price multiples in determining terminal value in a multistage discounted cash flow model.
- Discuss alternative definitions of cash flow used in price and enterprise value multiples (including enterprise value to earnings before interest, taxes, depreciation, and amortization) and explain the limitations of each.
- Discuss the sources of differences in cross-border valuation comparisons.
- Describe the main types of momentum indicators and their use in valuation.
- Explain the use of stock screens in investment management.

SUMMARY OVERVIEW

In this chapter, we have defined and explained the most important valuation indicators in professional use and illustrated their application to a variety of valuation problems.

- Price multiples are ratios of a stock's price to some measure of value per share.
- Price multiples are most frequently applied to valuation in the method of comparables. This method involves using a price multiple to evaluate whether an asset is relatively undervalued, fairly valued, or overvalued in relation to a benchmark value of the multiple.
- The benchmark value of the multiple may be the multiple of a similar company or the median or average value of the multiple for a peer group of companies, an industry, an economic sector, an equity index, or the company's own median or average past values of the multiple.
- The economic rationale for the method of comparables is the law of one price.
- Price multiples may also be applied to valuation in the method based on forecasted fundamentals. Discounted cash flow (DCF) models provide the basis and rationale for this method. Fundamentals also interest analysts who use the method of comparables because differences between a price multiple and its benchmark value may be explained by differences in fundamentals.
- The key idea behind the use of price-to-earnings ratios (P/Es) is that earning power is a chief driver of investment value and earnings per share (EPS) is probably the primary focus of security analysts' attention. The EPS figure, however, is frequently subject to distortion, often volatile, and sometimes negative.
- The two alternative definitions of P/E are trailing P/E, based on the most recent four quarters of EPS, and forward P/E, based on next year's expected earnings.
- Analysts address the problem of cyclicality by normalizing EPS—that is, calculating the level of EPS that the business could achieve currently under midcyclical conditions (normalized EPS).
- Two methods to normalize EPS are the method of historical average EPS (calculated over the most recent full cycle) and the method of average return on equity (ROE = average ROE multiplied by current book value per share).
- Earnings yield (E/P) is the reciprocal of the P/E. When stocks have zero or negative EPS, a ranking by earnings yield is meaningful whereas a ranking by P/E is not.
- Historical trailing P/Es should be calculated with EPS lagged a sufficient amount of time to avoid look-ahead bias. The same principle applies to other multiples calculated on a trailing basis.
- The fundamental drivers of P/E are the expected earnings growth rate and the required rate of return. The justified P/E based on fundamentals bears a positive relationship to the first factor and an inverse relationship to the second factor.

- PEG (P/E to growth) is a tool to incorporate the impact of earnings growth on P/E. PEG is calculated as the ratio of the P/E to the consensus growth forecast. Stocks with low PEGs are, all else equal, more attractive than stocks with high PEGs.
- We can estimate terminal value in multistage DCF models by using price multiples based on comparables. The expression for terminal value, V_n, is (using P/E as the example)

$$V_n = \text{Benchmark value of trailing P/E} \times E_n$$

or

$$V_n = \text{Benchmark value of forward P/E} \times E_{n+1}$$

- Book value per share is intended to represent, on a per-share basis, the investment that common shareholders have in the company. Inflation, technological change, and accounting distortions, however, may impair the use of book value for this purpose.
- Book value is calculated as common shareholders' equity divided by the number of shares outstanding. Analysts adjust book value to accurately reflect the value of the shareholders' investment and to make P/B (the price-to-book ratio) more useful for comparing different stocks.
- The fundamental drivers of P/B are ROE and the required rate of return. The justified P/B based on fundamentals bears a positive relationship to the first factor and an inverse relationship to the second factor.
- An important rationale for using the price-to-sales ratio (P/S) is that sales, as the top line in an income statement, are generally less subject to distortion or manipulation than other fundamentals, such as EPS or book value. Sales are also more stable than earnings and are never negative.
- P/S fails to take into account differences in cost structure between businesses, may not properly reflect the situation of companies losing money, and may be subject to manipulation through revenue recognition practices.
- The fundamental drivers of P/S are profit margin, growth rate, and the required rate of return. The justified P/S based on fundamentals bears a positive relationship to the first two factors and an inverse relationship to the third factor.
- Enterprise value (EV) is total company value (the market value of debt, common equity, and preferred equity) minus the value of cash and investments.
- The ratio of EV to total sales is conceptually preferable to P/S because EV/S facilitates comparisons among companies with varying capital structures.
- A key idea behind the use of price to cash flow is that cash flow is less subject to manipulation than are earnings. Price to cash flow multiples are often more stable than P/E. Some common approximations to cash flow from operations have limitations, however, because they ignore items that may be subject to manipulation.
- The major cash flow (and related) concepts used in multiples are earnings plus noncash charges (CF), cash flow from operations (CFO), free cash flow to equity (FCFE), and earnings before interest, taxes, depreciation, and amortization (EBITDA).
- In calculating price to cash flow, the earnings-plus-noncash-charges concept is traditionally used, although FCFE has the strongest link to financial theory.
- CF and EBITDA are not strictly cash flow numbers because they do not account for noncash revenue and net changes in working capital.
- The fundamental drivers of price to cash flow, however defined, are the expected growth rate of future cash flow and the required rate of return. The justified price to cash flow based on fundamentals bears a positive relationship to the first factor and an inverse relationship to the second.

- EV/EBITDA is preferred to P/EBITDA because EBITDA, as a pre-interest number, is a flow to all providers of capital.
- EV/EBITDA may be more appropriate than P/E for comparing companies with different amounts of financial leverage (debt).
- EV/EBITDA is frequently used in the valuation of capital-intensive businesses.
- The fundamental drivers of EV/EBITDA are the expected growth rate in free cash flow to the firm, profitability, and the weighted average cost of capital. The justified EV/EBITDA based on fundamentals bears a positive relationship to the first two factors and an inverse relationship to the third.
- Dividend yield has been used as a valuation indicator because it is a component of total return and is less risky than capital appreciation.
- Trailing dividend yield is calculated as four times the most recent quarterly per-share dividend divided by the current market price.
- The fundamental drivers of dividend yield are the expected growth rate in dividends and the required rate of return.
- Comparing companies across borders frequently involves dealing with differences in accounting methods, cultural differences, economic differences, and resulting differences in risk and growth opportunities.
- Momentum indicators relate either price or a fundamental to the time series of the price or fundamental's own past values (in some cases, to their expected values).
- Momentum valuation indicators include earnings surprise, standardized unexpected earnings (SUE), and relative strength.
- Unexpected earnings (or earnings surprise) equals the difference between reported earnings and expected earnings.
- SUE is unexpected earnings divided by the standard deviation in past unexpected earnings.
- Relative-strength indicators allow comparison of a stock's performance during a period either with its own past performance (first type) or with the performance of some group of stocks (second type). The rationale for using relative strength is the thesis that patterns of persistence or reversal in returns exist.
- Screening is the application of a set of criteria to reduce an investment universe to a smaller set of investments and is a part of many stock selection disciplines. In general, limitations of such screens include the lack of control in vendor-provided data of the calculation of important inputs and the absence of qualitative factors.

PROBLEMS

1. As of February 2008, you are researching Jonash International, a hypothetical company subject to cyclical demand for its services. Jonash shares closed at $57.98 on 2 February 2007. You believe the 2003–2006 period reasonably captures average profitability:

Measure	2007	2006	2005	2004	2003
EPS	E$3.03	$ 1.45	$ 0.23	$ 2.13	$ 2.55
BV per share	E$19.20	$16.21	$14.52	$13.17	$11.84
ROE	E16.0%	8.9%	1.6%	16.3%	21.8%

    A. Define normalized EPS.

    B. Calculate a normalized EPS for Jonash based on the method of historical average EPS and then calculate the P/E based on normalized EPS.

    C. Calculate a normalized EPS for Jonash based on the method of average ROE and the P/E based on normalized EPS.

2. An analyst plans to use P/E and the method of comparables as a basis for recommending purchasing shares of one of two peer-group companies in the business of manufacturing personal digital assistants. Neither company has been profitable to date, and neither is expected to have positive EPS over the next year. Data on the companies' prices, trailing EPS, and expected growth rates in sales (five-year compounded rates) are given in the following table:

Company	Price	Trailing EPS	P/E	Expected Growth (Sales)
Hand	$22	–$2.20	NM	45%
Somersault	$10	–$1.25	NM	40%

Unfortunately, because the earnings for both companies have been negative, their P/Es are not meaningful. On the basis of this information, address the following:

    A. Discuss how the analyst might make a relative valuation in this case.

    B. State which stock the analyst should recommend.

3. May Stewart, CFA, a retail analyst, is performing a P/E-based comparison of two hypothetical jewelry stores as of early 2009. She has the following data for Hallwhite Stores (HS) and Ruffany (RUF).

    • HS is priced at $44. RUF is priced at $22.50.

    • HS has a simple capital structure, earned $2.00 per share (basic and diluted) in 2008, and is expected to earn $2.20 (basic and diluted) in 2009.

    • RUF has a complex capital structure as a result of its outstanding stock options. Moreover, it had several unusual items that reduced its basic EPS in 2008 to $0.50 (versus the $0.75 that it earned in 2007).

    • For 2009, Stewart expects RUF to achieve net income of $30 million. RUF has 30 million shares outstanding and options outstanding for an additional 3,333,333 shares.

    A. Which P/E (trailing or forward) should Stewart use to compare the two companies' valuation?

    B. Which of the two stocks is relatively more attractive when valued on the basis of P/Es (assuming that all other factors are approximately the same for both stocks)?

4. You are researching the valuation of the stock of a company in the food-processing industry. Suppose you intend to use the mean value of the forward P/Es for the food-processing industry stocks as the benchmark value of the multiple. This mean P/E is 18.0. The forward or expected EPS for the next year for the stock you are studying is $2.00. You calculate $18.0 \times \$2.00 = \$36$, which you take to be the intrinsic value of the stock based only on the information given here. Comparing $36 with the stock's current market price of $30, you conclude the stock is undervalued.

    A. Give two reasons why your conclusion that the stock is undervalued may be in error.

    B. What additional information about the stock and the peer group would support your original conclusion?

5. Suppose an analyst uses an equity index as a comparison asset in valuing a stock. In making a decision to recommend purchase of an individual stock, which price multiple(s) would cause concern about the impact of potential overvaluation of the equity index?

6. Christie Johnson, CFA, has been assigned to analyze Sundanci. Johnson assumes that Sundanci's earnings and dividends will grow at a constant rate of 13 percent. Exhibits 6-1 and 6-2 provide financial statements for the most recent two years (2007 and 2008) and other information for Sundanci.

EXHIBIT 6-1   Sundanci Actual 2007 and 2008 Financial Statements for Fiscal Years Ending 31 May (in millions, except per-share data)

Income Statement	2007	2008
Revenue	$474	$598
Depreciation	20	23
Other operating costs	368	460
Income before taxes	86	115
Taxes	26	35
Net income	60	80
Dividends	18	24
Earnings per share	$0.714	$0.952
Dividends per share	$0.214	$0.286
Common shares outstanding	84.0	84.0
Balance Sheet	**2007**	**2008**
Current assets	$201	$326
Net property, plant, and equipment	474	489
Total assets	675	815
Current liabilities	57	141
Long-term debt	0	0
Total liabilities	57	141
Shareholders' equity	618	674
Total liabilities and equity	675	815
Other Information		
Capital expenditures	34	38

EXHIBIT 6-2   Selected Financial Information

Required rate of ROE	14%
Growth rate of industry	13%
Industry P/E	26

A. Based on information in Exhibits 6-1 and 6-2 and on Johnson's assumptions for Sundanci, calculate justified trailing and forward P/Es for this company.

B. Identify, within the context of the constant dividend growth model, how *each* of the following fundamental factors would affect the P/E:

   i.   The risk (beta) of Sundanci increases substantially.

   ii. The estimated growth rate of Sundanci's earnings and dividends increases.

   iii. The equity risk premium increases.

   Note: A change in a fundamental factor is assumed to happen in isolation; interactive effects between factors are ignored. That is, every other item of the company is unchanged.

7. Tom Smithfield is valuing the stock of a food-processing business. He feels confident explicitly projecting earnings and dividends to three years (to $t = 3$). Other information and estimates are as follows:

   - Required rate of return = 0.09
   - Average dividend payout rate for mature companies in the market = 0.45
   - Industry average ROE = 0.10
   - $E_3 = \$3.00$
   - Industry average P/E = 12

   On the basis of this information, answer the following questions:

   A. Compute terminal value (V_3) based on comparables.

   B. Contrast your answer in Part A to an estimate of terminal value based on the Gordon growth model.

8. Discuss three types of stocks or investment situations for which an analyst could appropriately use P/B in valuation.

9. Aratatech is a multinational distributor of semiconductor chips and related products to businesses. Its leading competitor around the world is Trymye Electronics. Aratatech has a current market price of $10.00, 20 million shares outstanding, annual sales of $1 billion, and a 5 percent profit margin. Trymye has a market price of $20.00, 30 million shares outstanding, annual sales of $1.6 billion, and a profit margin of 4.9 percent. Based on the information given, answer the following questions:

   A. Which of the two companies has a more attractive valuation based on P/S?

   B. Identify and explain one advantage of P/S over P/E as a valuation tool.

10. Wilhelm Müller, CFA, has organized the following selected data on four food companies (*TTM* stands for trailing 12 months):

Measure	Hoppelli Foods	Telli Foods	Drisket Co.	Whiteline Foods
Stock price	$25.70	$11.77	$23.65	$24.61
Shares outstanding (thousands)	138,923	220,662	108,170	103,803
Market cap ($ millions)	3,570	2,597	2,558	2,555
Enterprise value ($ millions)	3,779	4,056	3,846	4,258
Sales ($ millions)	4,124	10,751	17,388	6,354
Operating income ($ millions)	285	135	186	396
Operating profit margin	6.91%	1.26%	1.07%	6.23%

(*Continued*)

Measure	Hoppelli Foods	Telli Foods	Drisket Co.	Whiteline Foods
Net income ($ millions)	182	88	122	252
TTM EPS	$1.30	$0.40	$1.14	$2.43
Return on equity	19.20%	4.10%	6.40%	23.00%
Net profit margin	4.41%	0.82%	0.70%	3.97%

On the basis of the data given, answer the following questions:

A. Calculate the trailing P/E and EV/Sales for each company.

B. Explain, on the basis of fundamentals, why these stocks have different EV/S multiples.

11. John Jones, CFA, is head of the research department at Peninsular Research. Peninsular has a client who has inquired about the valuation method best suited for comparing companies in an industry with the following characteristics:

   • Principal competitors within the industry are located in the United States, France, Japan, and Brazil.

   • The industry is currently operating at a cyclical low, with many companies reporting losses.

   Jones recommends that the client consider the following valuation ratios:

   1. P/E
   2. P/B
   3. EV/S

   Determine which *one* of the three valuation ratios is most appropriate for comparing companies in this industry. Support your answer with *one* reason that makes that ratio superior to either of the other two ratios in this case.

12. Giantin Growing AG (GG) is currently selling for €38.50, with TTM EPS and dividends per share of €1.36 and €0.91, respectively. The company's P/E is 28.3, P/B is 7.1, and P/S is 2.9. The ROE is 27.0 percent, and the profit margin on sales is 10.24 percent. The Treasury bond rate is 4.9 percent, the equity risk premium is 5.5 percent, and GG's beta is 1.2.

   A. What is GG's required rate of return, based on the capital asset pricing model (CAPM)?

   B. Assume that the dividend and earnings growth rates are 9 percent. What trailing P/E, P/B, and P/S multiples would be justified in light of the required rate of return in part A and current values of the dividend payout ratio, ROE, and profit margin?

   C. Given that the assumptions and constant growth model are appropriate, state and justify whether GG, based on fundamentals, appears to be fairly valued, overvalued, or undervalued.

13. Jorge Zaldys, CFA, is researching the relative valuation of two companies in the aerospace/defense industry, NCI Heavy Industries (NCI) and Relay Group International (RGI). He has gathered relevant information on the companies in the following table.

EBITDA Comparisons (in € millions except per-share and share-count data)

Company	RGI	NCI
Price per share	150	100
Shares outstanding	5 million	2 million
Market value of debt	50	100
Book value of debt	52	112
Cash and investments	5	2
Net income	49.5	12
Net income from continuing operations	49.5	8
Interest expense	3	5
Depreciation and amortization	8	4
Taxes	2	3

Using the information in the table, answer the following questions:
A. Calculate P/EBITDA for NCI and RGI.
B. Calculate EV/EBITDA for NCI and RGI.
C. Which company should Zaldys recommend as relatively undervalued? Justify the selection.

14. Define the major alternative cash flow concepts, and state one limitation of each.

15. Data for two hypothetical companies in the pharmaceutical industry, DriveMed and MAT Technology, are given in the following table. For both companies, expenditures on fixed capital and working capital during the previous year reflect anticipated average expenditures over the foreseeable horizon.

Measure	DriveMed	MAT Technology
Current price	$46.00	$78.00
Trailing CF per share	$3.60	$6.00
P/CF	12.8	13.0
Trailing FCFE per share	$1.00	$5.00
P/FCFE	46.0	15.6
Consensus five-year growth forecast	15%	20%
Beta	1.25	1.25

On the basis of the information supplied, discuss the valuation of MAT Technology relative to DriveMed. Justify your conclusion.

16. Your value-oriented investment management firm recently hired a new analyst, Bob Westard, because of his expertise in the life sciences and biotechnology areas. At the firm's weekly meeting, during which each analyst proposes a stock idea for inclusion in the firm's approved list, Westard recommends Hitech Clothing International (HCI).

He bases his recommendation on two considerations. First, HCI has pending patent applications but a P/E that he judges to be low in light of the potential earnings from the patented products. Second, HCI has had high relative strength versus the S&P 500 over the past month.

A. Explain the difference between Westard's two approaches—that is, the use of price multiples and the relative-strength approach.

B. State which, if any, of the bases for Westard's recommendation is consistent with the investment orientation of your firm.

17. Kirstin Kruse, a portfolio manager, has an important client who wants to alter the composition of her equity portfolio, which is currently a diversified portfolio of 60 global common stocks. Because of concerns about the economy and based on the thesis that the consumer staples sector will be less hurt than others in a recession, the client wants to add a group of stocks from the consumer staples sector. In addition, the client wants the stocks to meet the following criteria:

- Stocks must be considered large cap (i.e., have a large market capitalization).
- Stocks must have a dividend yield of at least 4.0 percent.
- Stocks must have a forward P/E no greater than 15.

The following table shows how many stocks satisfied each screen, which was run in July 2008.

Screen	Number Satisfying
Consumer staples sector	277
Large cap (>$9.7 billion in this database)	446
Dividend yield of at least 4.0%	1,609
P/E less than 15	2,994
All four screens	6

The stocks meeting all four screens were Altria Group, Inc.; British American Tobacco (the company's ADR); Reynolds American, Inc.; Tesco PLC (the ADR); Unilever N.V. (the ADR); and Unilever PLC (the ADR).

A. Critique the construction of the screen.

B. Do these criteria identify appropriate additions to this client's portfolio?

CHAPTER 7

PRIVATE COMPANY VALUATION

LEARNING OUTCOMES

After completing this chapter, you will be able to do the following:

- Compare and contrast public and private company valuation.
- Identify and explain the reasons for valuing the total capital and/or equity capital of private businesses.
- Explain the role of definitions (standards) of value, explain the different definitions of value, and illustrate how different definitions can lead to different estimates of value.
- Discuss the three major approaches to private company valuation.
- Illustrate and explain the adjustments required to estimate the normalized earnings and/or cash flow for a private company, from the perspective of either a strategic or nonstrategic (financial) buyer and explain cash flow estimation issues.
- Explain and illustrate methods under the income approach to private company valuation including the free cash flow method, capitalized cash flow method, and excess earnings method.
- Identify and explain specific elements of discount rate estimation that are relevant in valuing the total capital or equity capital of a private business.
- Compare and contrast models used in a private company equity required rate of return estimation (including the CAPM, the expanded CAPM, and the build-up method) and discuss the issues related to using each.
- Discuss and illustrate market approaches to private company valuation, including the guideline public company method, the guideline transactions method, and the prior transaction method, and the advantages and disadvantages of each.
- Discuss and illustrate the asset-based approach to private company valuation.
- Discuss and illustrate the use of discounts and premiums in private company valuation.
- Explain the role of valuation standards in the valuation of private companies.

This chapter was contributed by Raymond D. Rath, ASA, CFA.

SUMMARY OVERVIEW

This chapter provides an overview of key elements of private company valuation and contrasts public and private company valuations.

- Company- and stock-specific factors may influence the selection of appropriate valuation methods and assumptions for private company valuations. Stock-specific factors may result in a lower value for an equity interest in a private company relative to a public company.
- Company-specific factors in which private companies differ from public companies include:
  - Stage in life cycle.
  - Size.
  - Overlap of shareholders and management.
  - Quality/depth of management.
  - Quality of financial and other information.
  - Pressure from short-term investors.
  - Tax concerns.
- Stock-specific factors that frequently affect the value of private companies include:
  - Liquidity of equity interests in business.
  - Concentration of control.
  - Potential agreements restricting liquidity.
- Private company valuations are typically performed for three different reasons: transactions, compliance (financial or tax reporting), or litigation. Acquisition-related valuation issues and financial reporting valuation issues are of greatest importance in assessing public companies.
- Different definitions (standards) of value exist. The use of a valuation and key elements pertaining to the appraised company will help determine the appropriate definition. Key definitions of value include:
  - Fair market value.
  - Market value.
  - Fair value for financial reporting.
  - Fair value in a litigation context.
  - Investment value.
  - Intrinsic value.
- Private company valuations may require adjustments to the income statements to develop estimates of the normalized earnings of the company. Adjustments may be required for nonrecurring, noneconomic, or other unusual items to eliminate anomalies and/or facilitate comparisons.
- Within the income approach, the free cash flow method is frequently used to value larger, mature private companies. For smaller companies or in special situations, the capitalized cash flow method and residual income method may also be used.
- Within the market approach, three methods are regularly used: the guideline public company method, guideline transactions method, and prior transactions method.
- An asset-based approach is infrequently used in the valuation of private companies. This approach may be appropriate for companies that are worth more in liquidation than as a going concern. This approach is also applied for asset holding companies, very small companies, or companies that were recently formed and have limited operating histories.

- Control and marketability issues are important and challenging elements in the valuation of private companies and equity interests therein.
- If publicly traded companies are used as the basis for pricing multiple(s), control premiums may be appropriate in measuring the value of the total equity of a private company. Control premiums have also been used to estimate lack of control discounts.
- Discounts for lack of control are used to convert a controlling interest value into a non-controlling equity interest value. Evidence of the adverse impact of the lack of control is an important consideration in assessing this discount.
- Discounts for lack of marketability (DLOMs) are often used in the valuation of noncontrolling equity interests in private companies. A DLOM may not be appropriate if there is a high likelihood of a liquidity event in the immediate future.
- Quantification of a DLOM can be challenging because of limited data, differences in the interpretation of available data, and different interpretations of the impact of the lack of marketability on a private company.
- DLOMs can be estimated based on (1) private sales of restricted stock in public companies relative to their freely traded share price, (2) private sales of stock in companies prior to a subsequent IPO, and (3) the pricing of put options.
- The intent of valuation standards is to protect users of valuations and the community at large. Standards typically cover the development and reporting of a valuation.
- A number of organizations have released valuation standards. No single set of valuation standards covers the valuation of private companies.

PROBLEMS

1. Two companies are considering the acquisition of Target Company. Buyer A is a strategic buyer and Buyer B is a financial buyer. The following information pertains to Target Company:
   - Sales = £28,000,000
   - Reported EBITDA = £4,500,000
   - Reported executive compensation = £1,000,000
   - Normalized executive compensation = £500,000
   - Reduced SG&A from eliminating duplicate general and administrative functions = £600,000

   Calculate the pro forma EBITDA estimates that the strategic and financial buyers would each develop in an acquisitions analysis of Target Company.

2. Using the build-up method and assuming that no adjustment for industry risk is required, calculate an equity discount rate for a small company, given the following information:
   - Equity risk premium = 5.0 percent
   - Mid-cap equity risk premium = 3.5 percent
   - Small stock risk premium = 4.2 percent
   - Income return on long-term bonds = 5.1 percent
   - Total return on intermediate-term bonds = 5.3 percent
   - Company-specific risk premium = 3.0 percent
   - 20-year Treasury bond yield as of the valuation date = 4.5 percent

3. Using the capitalized cash flow method (CCM), calculate the fair market value of 100 percent of the equity of a hypothetical company, given the following information:
   - Current year's reported free cash flow to equity = $1,400,000
   - Current year's normalized free cash flow to equity = $1,800,000
   - Long-term interest-bearing debt = $2,000,000
   - Weighted average cost of capital = 15 percent
   - Equity discount rate = 18 percent
   - Long-term growth rate of FCFE = 5.5 percent

4. You have been asked to value Pacific Corporation, Inc., using an excess earnings method, given the following information:
   - Working capital balance = $2,000,000
   - Fair value of fixed assets = $5,500,000
   - Book value of fixed assets = $4,000,000
   - Normalized earnings of firm = $1,000,000
   - Required return on working capital = 5.0 percent
   - Required return on fixed assets = 8.0 percent
   - Required return on intangible assets = 15.0 percent
   - Weighted average cost of capital = 10.0 percent
   - Long-term growth rate of residual income = 5.0 percent

   Based on this information:
   A. What is the value of Pacific's intangible assets?
   B. What is the market value of invested capital?

5. An appraiser has been asked to determine the combined level of valuation discounts for a small equity interest in a private company. The appraiser concluded that an appropriate control premium is 15 percent. A discount for lack of marketability was estimated at 25 percent. Given these factors, what is the combined discount?

The following information relates to Questions 6 through 11.

Alan Chin, the chief executive officer of Thunder Corporation, has asked his chief financial officer, Constance Ebinosa, to prepare a valuation of Thunder for the purpose of selling the company to a private investment partnership. Thunder is a profitable $200 million annual sales U.S. domiciled manufacturer of generic household products. Customers consist of several grocery store chains in the United States. Competitors include large companies such as Procter & Gamble, Clorox, and Unilever. Thunder has been in business for 15 years and is privately owned by the original shareholders, none of whom are employed by the company. The company's senior management has been in charge of the company's operations for most of the past 15 years and expects to remain in that capacity after any sale.

The partnership has expectations about Thunder similar to those of the current shareholders and management of Thunder. These investors expect to hold Thunder for an intermediate period of time and then bring the company public when market conditions are more favorable than currently.

Chin is concerned about what definition of value should be used when analyzing Thunder. He notes that the stock market has been very volatile recently. He also wonders whether fair market value can be realistically estimated when the most similar recent private market transactions may not have been at arm's length.

Chin asks Ebinosa whether there will be differences in the process of valuing a private company like Thunder compared with a public company. Ebinosa replies that differences do exist and mentions several factors an analyst must consider.

Ebinosa also explains that several approaches are available for valuing private companies. She mentions that one possibility is to use an asset-based approach because Thunder has a relatively large and efficient factory and warehouse for its products. A real estate appraiser can readily determine the value of these facilities. A second method would be the market approach and using an average of the price-to-earnings multiples for Procter & Gamble and Clorox. A third possibility is a discounted free cash flow approach. The latter would focus on a continuation of Thunder's trend of slow profitable growth during the past 10 years.

The private investment partnership has mentioned that they are likely to use an income approach as one of their methods. Ebinosa decides to validate the estimates they make. She assumes for the next 12 months that Thunder's revenues increase by the long-term annual growth rate of 3 percent. She also makes the following assumptions to calculate the free cash flow to the firm for the next 12 months:

- Gross profit margin is 45 percent.
- Depreciation is 2 percent of revenues.
- Selling, general, and administrative expenses are 24 percent of revenues.
- Capital expenditures equal 125 percent of depreciation to support the current level of revenues.
- Additional capital expenditures of 15 percent of incremental revenues are needed to fund future growth.
- Working capital investment equals 8 percent of incremental revenues.
- Marginal tax rate on EBIT is 35 percent.

Chin knows that if an income approach is used then the choice of discount rate may have a large influence on the estimated value. He makes two statements regarding discount rate estimates:

1. If the CAPM method is used to estimate the discount rate with a beta estimate based on public companies with operations and revenues similar to Thunder, then a small stock premium should be added to the estimate.
2. The weighted average cost of capital of the private investment partnership should be used to value Thunder.

Ebinosa decides to calculate a value of Thunder's equity using the capitalized cash flow method (CCM) and decides to use the build-up method to estimate Thunder's required return on equity. She makes the following assumptions:

- Growth of FCFE is at a constant annual rate of 3 percent.
- Free cash flow to equity for the year ahead is $2.5 million.
- Risk free rate is 4.5 percent.
- Equity risk premium is 5.0 percent.
- Size premium is 2.0 percent.

6. Given Chin's concerns, the *most appropriate* definition of value for Thunder is
   A. Intrinsic value.
   B. Investment value.
   C. Fair market value.

7. The *least likely* factor that would be a source of differences in valuing Thunder compared with valuing a publicly traded company is
   A. Access to public debt markets.
   B. Agency problems.
   C. The size of the company.

8. Ebinosa can best value Thunder using the
   A. Excess earnings approach.
   B. Asset-based approach.
   C. Discounted free cash flow approach.

9. The free cash flow to the firm is *closest* to
   A. $23,031,000.
   B. $25,441,000.
   C. $36,091,000.

10. Regarding the two statements about discount rate estimates, Chin is
    A. Correct with respect to adding the small stock premium and correct with respect to the weighted average cost of capital.
    B. Correct with respect to adding the small stock premium and incorrect with respect to the weighted average cost of capital.
    C. Incorrect with respect to adding the small stock premium and incorrect with respect to the weighted average cost of capital.

11. The indicated value of Thunder's equity using the build-up method and the capitalized cash flow method (CCM) based on free cash flow to equity is *closest* to
    A. $29.41 million.
    B. $38.46 million.
    C. $125.00 million.

The following information relates to Questions 12 through 17 (currency in Canadian dollars).

The senior vice president of acquisitions for Northland Industries, Angela Lanton, and her head analyst, Michael Powell, are evaluating several potential investments. Northland is a diversified holding company for numerous businesses. One of Northland's divisions is a manufacturer of fine papers and that division has alerted Lanton about Oakstar Timber, a supplier that may be available for purchase. Oakstar's sole owner, Felix Tanteromo, has expressed interest in exchanging his ownership of Oakstar for a combination of cash and Northland Industries securities.

Oakstar's main asset is 10,000 hectares of timberland in the western part of Canada. The land is a combination of new- and old-growth Douglas fir trees. The value of this timberland has been steadily increasing since Oakstar acquired it. Oakstar manages the land on a sustained yield basis (i.e., so it continues to produce timber indefinitely) and contracts with outside forestry companies to evaluate, harvest, and sell the timber. Oakstar's income is in the form of royalties (fees paid to Oakstar based on the number of cubic meters harvested). Oakstar's balance sheet as of 31 December 2008 is as follows.

Oakstar Timber Balance Sheet Year Ended 31 December 2008

Assets	
Cash	$ 500,000
Inventory	25,000
Accounts receivable	50,000
Plant and equipment (cost less depreciation)	750,000
Land	10,000,000
Total assets	$11,325,000
Liabilities and Equity	
Accounts payables	$ 75,000
Long-term bank loan	1,500,000
Common stock	9,750,000
Total liabilities and equity	$11,325,000

In addition to the balance sheet, Powell is gathering other data to assist in valuing Oakstar and has found information on recent sales of timberland in the western part of Canada. Douglas fir properties have averaged $6,178 per hectare for tracts that are not contiguous and do not have a developed road system for harvesting the timber. For tracts that have these features, as possessed by Oakstar, the average price is $8,750 per hectare. Properties near urban areas and having potential for residential and recreational second home development command up to $20,000 per hectare. Oakstar's land lacks this potential. Lanton believes these values would form the basis of an asset-based valuation for Oakstar, with the additional assumption that other assets and liabilities on the balance sheet are assumed to be worth their stated values.

The second company under evaluation, FAMCO, Inc., is a family-owned electronic manufacturing company with annual sales of $120 million. The family wants to monetize the value of their ownership in FAMCO with a view to later investing part of the proceeds in a diversified stock portfolio. Lanton has asked Powell to obtain data for both an income-based and market-based valuation. Powell has obtained the recent annual income statement and additional data needed to calculate normalized earnings as follows.

FAMCO, Inc. Income Statement Year Ending 31 December 2008

Revenues		$120,000,000
Gross profit		85,000,000
Selling, general, and administrative expenses		23,000,000
Pro forma EBITDA		$ 62,000,000
Depreciation and amortization		3,500,000
Pro forma earnings before interest and taxes		$ 58,500,000
Less: Interest		1,000,000
Earnings before taxes (EBT)		$ 57,500,000
Pro forma taxes on EBT	40%	23,000,000
Operating income after tax		$ 34,500,000

Additional data for FAMCO is provided in the following table. Included are estimates by Powell of the compensation paid to family members and the smaller amount of salary expense for replacement employees if Northland acquires the company (reflecting perceived above-market compensation of the family group executives). He believes the current debt of FAMCO can be replaced with a more optimal level of debt at a lower interest rate. These will be reflected in a normalized income statement.

FAMCO, Inc.	
Current debt level	$10,000,000
Current interest rate	10%
Salaries of employed family members	$7,000,000
Salaries of replacement employees	$5,400,000
New debt level	$25,000,000
New interest rate	8%

Powell also recognizes that a value needs to be assigned to FAMCO's intangibles consisting of patents and other intangible assets. Powell prepares an additional estimate of excess earnings and intangibles value using the capitalized cash flow method. He gathers the following data:

FAMCO, Inc.—Intangibles Valuation Data	
Working capital balance	$10,000,000
Fair value of fixed assets	$45,000,000
Normalized income to the company	$35,000,000
Required return on working capital	8%
Required return on fixed assets	12%
Required return on intangible assets	20%
Weighted average cost of capital	14.5%
Future growth rate	6%

Lanton asks Powell to also use the market approach to valuation with a focus on the guideline transactions method. Powell prepares a table showing relevant information regarding three recent guideline transactions and market conditions at the time of the transactions. Powell's assumptions about FAMCO include its expected fast growth and moderate level of risk.

Target firm	Target's risk	Target's growth	Consideration	Market conditions
Firm 1	High	Slow	Cash	Normal, rising trend
Firm 2	Moderate	Fast	Stock	Prices near peak
Firm 3	Moderate	Fast	Cash	Normal, rising trend

Although Northland is interested in acquiring all of the stock of FAMCO, the acquisition of a 15 percent equity interest in FAMCO is also an option. Lanton asks Powell about the valuation of small equity interests in private entities and notes that control and marketability are important factors that lead to adjustments in value estimates for small equity interests. Powell mentions that the control premium paid for the most similar guideline firm used in the analysis suggests a discount for lack of control of 20 percent. The discount for lack of marketability was estimated at 15 percent.

12. Which of the following statements concerning asset-based valuation as applied to Oakstar is *most* accurate? The approach is applicable
    A. Only when a guideline public company for the valuation is not available.
    B. Because natural resources with determinable market values constitute the majority of Oakstar's total value.
    C. Because as a passive collector of royalties, Oakstar has no meaningful capital expenditures and free cash flow is irrelevant.

13. Using an asset-based approach, the value (net of debt) of Oakstar is *closest* to
    A. $62,250,000.
    B. $87,250,000.
    C. $199,750,000.

14. The normalized earnings after tax for FAMCO is *closest* to
    A. $32,940,000.
    B. $34,260,000.
    C. $34,860,000.

15. Using the excess earnings method, the value of the intangibles is *closest* to
    A. $144.0 million.
    B. $205.7 million.
    C. $338.8 million.

16. The guideline transaction that is *most likely* applicable to FAMCO is
    A. Firm 1.
    B. Firm 2.
    C. Firm 3.

17. The total discount for both control and marketability is *closest* to
    A. 15 percent.
    B. 32 percent.
    C. 35 percent.

PART II

SOLUTIONS

CHAPTER 1

EQUITY VALUATION: APPLICATIONS AND PROCESSES

SOLUTIONS

1. The statement is flawed in at least two ways. First, active investors believe that stock prices do not always accurately reflect all relevant information on the security; for such investors, knowledge of equity valuation models is important for identifying investment opportunities because they represent a way to translate the investor's forecasts into value estimates for comparison with market prices. Thus, the "all" in "all investors" is misleading. Second, not all equities are publicly traded and have market prices, and the most recent market price can be stale for the many public equities that trade only infrequently.

2. No matter how diligent the analyst, some uncertainty always exists concerning (1) the accuracy of the analyst's forecasts and (2) whether an intrinsic value estimate accounts for all sources of risk reflected in market price. Thus, knowledge of a stock's investment characteristics is always incomplete. The practical consequences are that an investor can only estimate intrinsic value, and active security selection carries the risk of making mistakes in estimating value.

3. A. Liquidation value is typically not relevant to estimating intrinsic value for profitable companies because, in general, value would be destroyed by selling such a company's assets individually. Stated another way, the value added by being a going concern is a relevant investment characteristic that an intrinsic value estimate would recognize.

   B. A going-concern assumption generally increases the value placed on a company's inventory relative to not making that assumption. Usually, inventory that can be sold in the company's regular distribution channels would realize higher amounts than inventory that must be sold immediately because a company is being liquidated.

4. The key difference is that for inferring investor expectations the market price is used as the model input for value, whereas for obtaining an independent estimate of value, value is left as the unknown in the model. In the latter case, value is estimated based on the analyst's estimates for the variables that determine value.

5. Consider the present value of a single cash flow. If one increased the discount rate, one would also need to increase the cash flow if a constant present value were to be maintained. By a similar argument, if Cornell had used a higher discount rate, he would have needed to project a higher level of assumed future cash flows than he did for their present value to have been consistent with the given preannouncement price of $61.50. Thus, the implied growth rate consistent with a price of $61.50 would have been higher than the 20 percent growth rate estimated by Cornell.

6. An understanding of the company's business facilitates a focus on the key business aspects that affect value and, from a practical perspective, highlights the critical inputs to a forecast that should be tested using sensitivity analysis.

7. You need to know (1) the time horizon for the price target and (2) the required rate of return on MFG. The price target of €9.20 represents a potential 20 percent return from investing in the stock if the time horizon is one year, calculated as $(€9.20 + €0.05)/€7.73 - 1.0 = 0.197$; without a time frame, however, you cannot evaluate the attractiveness of that return. Given that the time frame for the return is established, you need to have an estimate of the required rate of return over the same time horizon.

   If the expected return of 19.7 percent exceeds the security's required return for the same horizon—in other words, if the share's expected alpha is positive—then MFG would appear to be undervalued.

8. A. Accelerating the payment of expenses reduces the acquired companies' last reported preacquisition cash flow. Accelerating expense recognition reduces the acquired companies' last reported preacquisition earnings. XMI's cash flow and earnings growth rates following the acquisitions would be expected to be biased upwards because of the depressed levels for the acquirees.

   B. That is an example of a relative valuation model (or the method of comparables), which compares a company's market multiple to the multiples of similar companies.

CHAPTER 2

RETURN CONCEPTS

SOLUTIONS

1. A. The expected holding was one year. The actual holding period was from 15 October 2007 to 5 November 2007, which is three weeks.
   B. Given fair pricing, the expected return equals the required return, 8.7 percent. The expected price appreciation return over the initial anticipated one-year holding period must be equal to the required return minus the dividend yield, which is 2.11/72.08 = 0.0293 or 2.93 percent. Thus expected price appreciation return was 8.7% – 2.93% = 5.77 percent.
   C. The realized return was ($69.52 – $72.08)/$72.08 = –0.03552 or –3.55 percent over three weeks. There was no dividend yield return over the actual holding period.
   D. The required return over a three-week holding period was $(1.00161)^3 – 1 = 0.484$ percent. Using the answer to C, the realized alpha was –3.552 – 0.484 = –4.036 percent or –4.04 percent.

2. For AOL Time Warner, the required return is

   $$r = R_F + \beta[E(R_M) – R_F] = 4.35\% + 2.50(8.04\%) = 4.35\% + 20.10\% = 24.45\%$$

   For J.P. Morgan Chase, the required return is

   $$r = R_F + \beta[E(R_M) – R_F] = 4.35\% + 1.50(8.04\%) = 4.35\% + 12.06\% = 16.41\%$$

   For Boeing, the required return is

   $$r = R_F + \beta[E(R_M) – R_F] = 4.35\% + 0.80(8.04\%) = 4.35\% + 6.43\% = 10.78\%$$

3. A. The Fama-French Model gives the required return as

   > r = T-bill rate + (Sensitivity to equity market factor × Equity risk premium)
   > + (Sensitivity to size factor × Size risk premium) + (Sensitivity to value factor
   > × Value risk premium)

   For TerraNova Energy, the required return is

   $$r = 4.7\% + (1.20 \times 4.5\%) + (–0.50 \times 2.7\%) + (–0.15 \times 4.3\%)$$
   $$= 4.7\% + 5.4\% – 1.35\% – 0.645\%$$
   $$= 8.1\%$$

   B. TerraNova Energy appears to be a large-cap, growth-oriented, high market risk stock as indicated by its negative size beta, negative value beta, and market beta above 1.0.

4. The required return is given by

$$r = 0.045 + (-0.2)(0.075) = 4.5\% - 1.5\% = 3.0\%$$

This example indicates that Newmont Mining has a required return of 3 percent. When beta is negative, an asset has a CAPM required rate of return that is below the risk-free rate. Cases of equities with negative betas are relatively rare.

5. B is correct. The Fama-French Model incorporates market, size, and value risk factors. One possible interpretation of the value risk factor is that it relates to financial distress.

6. Larsen & Toubro Ltd.'s WACC is 13.64 percent calculated as follows:

	Equity	Debt		WACC
Weight	0.80	0.20		
After-tax cost	15.6%	(1 – 0.30)8.28%		
Weight × Cost	12.48%	+ 1.16%	=	13.64%

7. A is correct. The backfilling of index returns using companies that have survived to the index construction date is expected to introduce a positive survivorship bias into returns.

8. B is correct. The events of 2004 to 2006 depressed share returns but (1) are not a persistent feature of the stock market environment, (2) were not offset by other positive events within the historical record, and (3) have led to relatively low valuation levels, which are expected to rebound.

9. A is correct. The required return reflects the magnitude of the historical equity risk premium, which is generally higher when based on a short-term interest rate (as a result of the normal upward-sloping yield curve), and the current value of the rate being used to represent the risk-free rate. The short-term rate is currently higher than the long-term rate, which will also increase the required return estimate. The short-term interest rate, however, overstates the long-term expected inflation rate. Using the short-term interest rate, estimates of the long-term required return on equity will be biased upwards.

10. C is correct. According to this model, the equity risk premium is computed as

Equity risk premium = {[(1 + EINFL)(1 + EGREPS)(1 + EGPE) – 1.0] + EINC}
      – Expected risk-free return

Here:

   EINFL = 4 percent per year (long-term forecast of inflation)

   EGREPS = 5 percent per year (growth in real earnings)

   EGPE = 1 percent per year (growth in market P/E ratio)

   EINC = 1 percent per year (dividend yield or the income portion)

   Risk-free return = 7 percent per year (for 10-year maturities)

By substitution, we get:

$$\{[(1.04)(1.05)(1.01) - 1.0] + 0.01\} - 0.07 = 0.113 - 0.07$$
$$= 0.043 \text{ or } 4.3\%$$

11. C is correct. Based on a long-term government bond yield of 7 percent, a beta of 1, and any of the risk premium estimates that can be calculated from the givens (e.g., a 2 percent historical risk premium estimate or 4.3 percent supply-side equity risk premium

estimate), the required rate of return would be at least 9 percent. Based on using a short-term rate of 9 percent, C is the correct choice.

12. B is correct. All else equal, the first issue's greater liquidity would tend to make its required return lower than the second issue's. However, the required return on equity increases as leverage increases. The first issue's higher required return must result from its higher leverage, more than offsetting the effect of its greater liquidity, given that both issues have the same market risk.

CHAPTER 3

DISCOUNTED DIVIDEND VALUATION

SOLUTIONS

1. Both companies are dividend-paying and have an established history of dividend payments that can provide some help in forecasting future dividends. In the case of GE, EPS has been increasing steadily from 2000 to 2007 and DPS has shown increases consistent with this trend. For example, EPS increased by $0.23 from 2005 to 2006 and DPS increased by $0.12. Then EPS increased by $0.18 from 2006 to 2007 and DPS increased by $0.12. The payout ratios have also been increasing gradually during the period examined. Dividends appear to be at least somewhat predictable given earnings forecasts. Overall, the DDM seems to be an appropriate model for valuing GE. In the case of GM, however, dividends do not have a discernable relationship to the company's profitability. For example, DPS was $2 in 2000 when GM was doing well and had an EPS of $6.68, but DPS continued to be $2 in 2005 when EPS was –$18.50. The company continued to pay dividends in 2007, which was the third consecutive year of a negative EPS: in 2007, EPS had fallen to –$68.45. The lack of a clear relationship of dividends to operating results suggests that the DDM is not appropriate for valuing GM.

2. A. Discounting the expected dividend of £5 in 2010 and the expected stock price of £250 at the end of 2010,

$$V_1 = \frac{D_2 + P_2}{(1+r)^1} = \frac{5 + 250}{(1+0.11)^1} = \frac{255}{1.11} = 229.73$$

   B. One way to answer this question is to use a DDM for two holding periods. Accordingly, discounting the expected dividend of £5 in 2010 and the expected stock price of £250 at the end of 2010 for two periods, and discounting the expected dividend of £4 in 2009 for one period,

$$V_0 = \frac{D_1}{(1+r)^1} + \frac{D_2 + P_2}{(1+r)^2} = \frac{4}{(1+0.11)^1} + \frac{5+250}{(1+0.11)^2}$$

$$= \frac{4}{1.11} + \frac{255}{1.11^2} = 3.60 + 206.96 = 210.57$$

   based on full precision, or £210.56 with intermediate rounding. Another way to answer this question is to use the answer to Part A and a DDM for one holding period. Accordingly, discounting the expected dividend of £4 in 2009 and the expected stock price of £229.73 at the end of 2009 for one period,

$$V_0 = \frac{D_1 + V_1}{(1+r)^1} = \frac{4 + 229.73}{(1+0.11)^1} = \frac{233.73}{1.11} = 210.57$$

3. A. The growth rate from 2005 to 2007 is $(15.50/9)^{1/2} - 1 = 0.312$ or 31.2 percent. The consensus predicted growth rate from 2007 to 2009 is $(20.20/15.50)^{1/2} - 1 = 0.142$ or 14.2 percent. Thus, the consensus forecast is for a sharp decline in the dividend growth rate for 2008 to 2009.

   B. Half of the growth rate computed in Part A = $14.2/2 = 7.1$ percent. Based on this growth rate, $D_1 = £15.50(1.071) = £16.60$, rounded. Using the Gordon growth model,

$$V_0 = \frac{D_1}{r-g} = \frac{16.60}{0.11 - 0.071} = 425.64$$

   or 425.65 based on not rounding the numerator.

   C. The estimated value of BSY would decrease as r increases and increase as g increases, all else equal.

4. Applying the Gordon growth model with the assumed 5.9 percent dividend growth rate results in an estimated value of $1,398.38 trillion for the S&P 500 Index.

$$V_0 = \frac{D_1}{r-g} = \frac{27.73(1+0.059)}{0.08 - 0.059} = \$1,398.38 \text{ trillion}$$

5. The preferred stock pays 4.5 percent of $100 or $4.50 in annual dividends. The dividend is fixed; so $g = 0$. Therefore, using the Gordon growth model with zero growth,

$$V_0 = \frac{D_1}{g} = \frac{4.50}{0.056} = \$80.36$$

6. This problem can be addressed using the Gordon growth model with constant expected negative growth. The estimated value of the stock is

$$V_0 = \frac{D_1}{r-g} = \frac{4}{0.11 - (-0.08)} = 21.05$$

7. Using the CAPM, the required rate of return on Maspeth Robotics shares is 4 percent + 1.2(5%) = 10 percent. Therefore, the constant dividend growth rate implied by a market price of €24 is 5.6 percent, as shown:

$$V_0 = \frac{D_0(1+g)}{r-g}$$

$$24 = \frac{1.00(1+g)}{0.10 - g}$$

$$2.4 - 24g = 1.00 + g$$

$$25g = 1.4$$

$$g = 0.056 \text{ or } 5.6 \text{ percent}$$

8. A. With $b = 0.60$, the dividend payout ratio is $1 - b = 1 - 0.60 = 0.40$.
     Sustainable growth rate $g = b(ROE) = 0.60(0.14) = 0.084$ or 8.4 percent.
   B. The company paid a dividend per share of $b(EPS) = 0.40(\$2) = \$0.80$ in 2008. The estimated value at the beginning of 2009 is

$$V_0 = \frac{D_1}{r - g} = \frac{0.80(1 + 0.0840)}{0.1100 - 0.0840} = \$33.35$$

   C. If the company was a no-growth company, that is, it paid out all its earnings and did not reinvest any, its earnings would stay the same. The value of such a company would be the value of a perpetuity, which is $D/r = E/r = \$2/0.11 = \$18.18$. This amount is the no-growth value per share. Therefore, PVGO $= \$33.35 - \$18.18 = \$15.17$.
   D. The fraction of the company's value that comes from its growth opportunities is $15.17/33.35 = 0.4549$ or 45.49 percent.

9. The payout ratio is A\$0.70/A\$2.00 $= 0.35 = 1 - b$, where b is the earnings retention ratio. Therefore, the justified trailing P/E based on fundamentals is 10.45, as shown:

$$\frac{P_0}{E_0} = \frac{(1 - b)(1 + g)}{r - g}$$
$$= \frac{0.35(1 + 0.045)}{0.08 - 0.045}$$
$$= 10.45$$

Because the market trailing P/E of 14 is greater than 10.45, Stellar Baking Company shares appear to be overvalued (i.e., selling at a higher than warranted P/E).

10. The dividends in stages 2 and 3 can be valued with the H-model, which estimates their value at the beginning of stage 2. In this case, V_6 would capture the value of stages 2 and 3 dividends. V_6 would then be discounted to the present. Also, the present values of dividends D_1 through D_6 need to be added to the present value of V_6.

$$V_6 = \frac{D_6(1 + g_L) + D_6 H(g_S - g_L)}{r - g_L}$$

where

$D_6 = D_0 (1 + g_S)^6 = 9(1.14)^6 = 19.7548$
$r = 0.16$
$H = 10/2 = 5$
$g_S = 0.14$
$g_L = 0.10$

$$V_6 = \frac{19.7548(1.10) + 19.7548(5)(0.14 - 0.10)}{0.16 - 0.10} = 428.02$$

PV of $V_6 = 428.02/1.16^6 = 175.68$

PV of $D_1 = 9(1.14)/1.16 = 8.8448$
PV of $D_2 = 9(1.14)^2/1.16^2 = 8.6923$
PV of $D_3 = 9(1.14)^3/1.16^3 = 8.5425$
PV of $D_4 = 9(1.14)^4/1.16^4 = 8.3952$
PV of $D_5 = 9(1.14)^5/1.16^5 = 8.2504$
PV of $D_6 = 9(1.14)^6/1.16^6 = 8.1082$

Value of stock $= 8.8448 + 8.6923 + 8.5425 + 8.3952 + 8.2504 + 8.1082 + 175.68$
$= $ Rs. 226.51

11. A. Let r be the required rate of return. Also let $t = 0$ indicate the middle of 2008. Because the dividend growth rate becomes constant from the middle of 2011 ($t = 3$), the value of the mature phase can be expressed as

$$V_3 = D_4/(r - g) = D_4/(r - 0.08)$$

Also,

$D_1 = 0.27(1.10) = 0.2970$
$D_2 = 0.27(1.10)^2 = 0.3267$
$D_3 = 0.27(1.10)^3 = 0.3594$
$D_4 = D_3(1.08) = 0.3594(1.08) = 0.3881$

V_0 can be expressed as

$$V_0 = 9.74 = \frac{D_1}{1+r} + \frac{D_2}{(1+r)^2} + \frac{D_3}{(1+r)^3} + \frac{V_3}{(1+r)^3}$$

$$= \frac{0.2970}{1 + 0.12} + \frac{0.3267}{(1 + 0.12)^2} + \frac{0.3594}{(1 + 0.12)^3} + \frac{0.3881}{(0.12 - 0.08)(1 + 0.12)^3}$$

$$= 0.2652 + 0.2604 + 0.2558 + 6.9064$$

A$ $= 7.69$

B. Because ANN's estimated value of A\$7.69 is less than the market price of A\$9.74, ANN appears to be overvalued at the market price.

12. A. Use the H-model expression, with $H = 6/2 = 3$ and long-term and short-term dividend growth rates of 0.05 and 0.10, respectively, which gives an expected return of 7.4 percent as shown:

$$r = \left(\frac{D_0}{P_0}\right)\left[(1 + g_L) + H(g_S - g_L)\right] + g_L$$

$$= 0.02\left[(1 + 0.05) + 3(0.10 - 0.05)\right] + 0.05$$

$$= 0.024 + 0.05$$

$$= 0.074$$

B. In this case the long- and short-term dividend growth rates are identical and the expected return is lower:

$$r = \left(\frac{D_0}{P_0}\right)\left[(1 + g_L) + H(g_s - g_L)\right] + g_L$$

$$= 0.02\left[(1 + 0.05) + 3(0.05 - 0.05)\right] + 0.05$$

$$= 0.021 + 0.05$$

$$= 0.071$$

It is intuitive that a higher dividend growth rate is associated with a higher expected return if all the other facts (such as the assumed required rate of return) are held constant.

13. A. The formula for sustainable growth rate is

$$g = (b \text{ in the mature phase}) \times (\text{ROE in the mature phase})$$

Because the dividend payout ratio in the mature phase is estimated to be 40 percent or 0.40, the retention ratio b is expected to $1 - 0.40 = 0.60$. Therefore, given the 11 percent per year forecasted ROE,

$$g = 0.60(11\%) = 6.6\%$$

B. Based on the formula for sustainable growth rate, as b increases, growth rate increases, holding all else constant. However, all else may not be constant. In particular, the return accruing to additional investments may be lower, leading to a lower overall ROE. If that is the case and Brother lowers the payout ratio to below 0.40 (thus increasing b to above 0.60), ROE would be expected to decline, which may lead to a lower growth rate.

14. A. The four components of PRAT are computed for 2007 as follows.
    P (Profit margin) = NI/Sales = 18,688/214,091 = 0.0873
    R (Retention) = b = (EPS − DPS)/EPS = (8.77 − 2.26)/8.77 = 0.7423
    A (Asset turnover) = Sales/Average total assets = 214,091/0.5(148,786 + 132,628)
                                = 1.5215
    T(Leverage) = Average total assets/Average shareholders' equity
                = (148,786 + 132,628)/(77,088 + 68,935) = 1.9272

The components are similarly computed for the other years and summarized in the following table. Their average values are also included.

Item	Needed for Solution to B Average	Solution to A 2007	2006	2005
P (Profit margin)	0.0812	0.0873	0.0836	0.0728
R (Retention)	0.7390	0.7423	0.7423	0.7324
A (Asset turnover)	1.6250	1.5215	1.5855	1.7681
T (Leverage)	1.9736	1.9272	1.9638	2.0299

B. Using the average values for each component,

$$g = \text{PRAT} = (0.0812)(0.7390)(1.6250)(1.9736) = 0.1924 \text{ or } 19.2 \text{ percent}$$

The sustainable growth rate for Chevron based on the PRAT expression is 19.8 percent.

C. Given that the high value of g does not seem sustainable indefinitely, it appears that the company has not reached the mature phase yet.

15. A. The following table provides the details from the spreadsheet model. The constant growth rate after year 4 is 2 percent less than that in year 4. Therefore,

$$g = 0.1180 - 0.0200 = 0.098 \text{ or } 9.8 \text{ percent}$$
$$V_4 = D_4(1+g)/(r-g) = 1.80(1.098)/(0.13 - 0.098) = \$61.76$$

Year	1	2	3	4
Sales ($ millions)	300.00	345.00	396.75	436.43
EBIT	51.00	58.65	67.45	74.19
Interest (%)	10.00	10.00	10.00	10.00
EBT	41.00	48.65	57.45	64.19
Taxes (30%)	12.30	14.60	17.23	19.26
Net income	28.70	34.06	40.21	44.93
Dividends	11.48	13.62	16.09	17.97
DPS	1.15	1.36	1.61	1.80
Growth rate of DPS		18.26%	18.38%	11.80%
PV of DPS	1.02	1.07	1.12	1.10
$V_4 = D_4(1+g)/(r-g)$				61.76
PV of V_4				$37.87

B. V_0 = Sum of PV of DPS and PV of V_4 = $1.02 + 1.07 + 1.12 + 1.10 + 61.76/(1 + 0.13)^4 = \$42.18$.

C. The following table provides the details if the sales growth rate in year 3 is 10 percent.

Year	1	2	3	4
Sales ($ millions)	300.00	345.00	379.50	417.45
EBIT	51.00	58.65	64.52	70.97
Interest (%)	10.00	10.00	10.00	10.00
EBT	41.00	48.65	54.52	60.97
Taxes (%)	12.30	14.60	16.35	18.29
Net income	28.70	34.06	38.16	42.68
Dividends	11.48	13.62	15.26	17.07
DPS	1.15	1.36	1.53	1.71
Growth rate of DPS		18.26%	12.50%	11.76%
PV of DPS	1.02	1.07	1.06	1.05
$V_4 = D_4(1+g)/(r-g)$				57.93
PV of V_4				$35.53

V_0 = Sum of PV of DPS and PV of V_4 = $39.73

16. C is correct. Using the Gordon growth model,

$$V_0 = \frac{D_1}{r-g} = \frac{0.59(1+0.0530)}{0.1115 - 0.0530} = \$10.62$$

17. A is correct. The justified trailing P/E or P_0/E_0 is V_0/E_0, where V_0 is the fair value based on the stock's fundamentals. The fair value V_0 computed earlier is \$10.62 and E_0 is \$2.12. Therefore, the justified trailing P/E is 10.62/2.12 = 5.01.

18. A is correct. Rae's estimate of the intrinsic value is \$10.62. Thus, the band Rae is looking at is \$10.62 ± 0.10(\$10.62), which runs from \$10.62 + \$1.06 = \$11.68 on the upside to \$10.62 – \$1.06 = \$9.56 on the downside. Because \$8.42 is below \$9.56, Rae would consider Tasty Foods to be undervalued.

19. B is correct. Using a beta of 1.25, Rae's estimate for the required return on equity for Tasty Foods is 0.04 + 1.25(0.065) = 0.1213 or 12.13 percent. The estimated value of the stock is

$$V_0 = \frac{D_1}{r-g} = \frac{0.59 \times (1+0.0530)}{0.1213 - 0.0530} = \$9.10$$

20. A is correct. The price of the stock is \$8.42. If this price is also the fair value of the stock,

$$V_0 = 8.42 = \frac{D_1}{r-g} = \frac{0.59 \times (1+g)}{0.1115 - g}$$

$$0.9388 - 8.42g = 0.59 + 0.59g$$

$$9.01g = 0.3488$$

$$g = 0.0387 \text{ or } 3.87 \text{ percent}$$

21. A is correct. If the stock is fairly priced in the market as per the Gordon growth model, the stock price is expected to increase at g, the expected growth rate in dividends. The implied growth rate in dividends, if price is the fair value, is 3.87 percent. Therefore, the expected capital gains yield is 3.87 percent.

22. B is correct. The following table provides the calculations needed to compute the value of the stock using the first approach, including the calculations for the terminal value V_8. As the table shows, the terminal value V_8 = C\$31.0550.

Time	Value	Calculation	D_t or V_t	Present Values $D_t/(1.0872)^t$ or $V_t/(1.0872)^t$
1	D_1	C\$0.175(1.14)	C\$0.1995	C\$0.1835
2	D_2	$0.175(1.14)^2$	0.2274	0.1924
3	D_3	$0.175(1.14)^3$	0.2593	0.2018
4	D_4	$0.175(1.14)^4$	0.2956	0.2116
5	D_5	$0.175(1.14)^5$	0.3369	0.2218
6	D_6	$0.175(1.14)^6$	0.3841	0.2326
7	D_7	$0.175(1.14)^7$	0.4379	0.2439
8	D_8	$0.175(1.14)^8$	0.4992	0.2557
8	V_8	$0.175(1.14)^8(1.07)/$ $(0.0872-0.07)$	31.0550	15.9095
Total				C\$17.6528

23. C is correct. As shown in the preceding table, the value of the second stage = PV of V_8 = C\$15.9095. The total value is C\$17.6528. As a proportion, the second stage represents $15.9095/17.6528 = 0.90$ of the total value.

24. B is correct.

$$V_8/E_8 = 17$$

$$D_8/E_8 = 1 - 0.70 = 0.30$$

From the table with the calculation details for the solution to problem 22, D_8 = C\$0.4992. Therefore, $0.4992/E_8 = 0.30$, which means that $E_8 = 0.4992/0.30 = 1.6640$.

$$V_8/E_8 = 17$$

implies that $V_8/1.6640 = 17$, which gives

$$V_8 = 17(1.6640) = C\$28.2880$$

25. A is correct. As computed earlier, $V_8 = 17(1.6640) = C\$28.2880$.

$$\text{PV of } V_8 = 28.2880/1.0872^8 = 14.4919$$

From the table with the calculation details for the solution to problem 22,

$$\text{Sum of PV of } D_1 \text{ through } D_8 = 1.7433$$

Therefore, the value of stock $V_0 = 14.4919 + 1.7433 = C\$16.2352$.

26. C is correct: Using the H-model

$$V_0 = \frac{D_0(1 + g_L) + D_0 H(g_S - g_L)}{r - g_L}$$

where

$$D_0 = 0.175$$
$$r = 0.0872$$
$$H = 4$$
$$g_S = 0.14$$
$$g_L = 0.07$$

$$V_0 = \frac{0.175(1.07) + 0.175(4)(0.14 - 0.07)}{0.0872 - 0.07} = 13.7355$$

The market price is C\$17, which is greater than C\$13.7355. Therefore, the stock is overvalued in the market.

27. B is correct. If the extraordinary growth rate of 14 percent is expected to continue for a longer duration, the stock's value would increase. Choice A is false because given that the first stage is longer (11 years instead of 8), the terminal value is being calculated at a later point in time. Therefore, its present value would be smaller. Moreover, the first stage has more years and contributes more to the total value. Overall, the proportion contributed by the second stage would be smaller. Choice C is false because the intrinsic value of the stock would be higher and the appropriate conclusion would be that the stock would be undervalued to a greater extent based on the first approach.

CHAPTER 4

FREE CASH FLOW VALUATION

SOLUTIONS

1.

For a $100 increase in:	Change in FCFF (in U.S. dollars)	Change in FCFE (in U.S. dollars)
A. Net income	+100	+100
B. Cash operating expenses	−60	−60
C. Depreciation	+40	+40
D. Interest expense	0	−60
E. EBIT	+60	+60
F. Accounts receivable	−100	−100
G. Accounts payable	+100	+100
H. Property, plant, and equipment	−100	−100
I. Notes payable	0	+100
J. Cash dividends paid	0	0
K. Proceeds from new shares issued	0	0
L. Common shares repurchased	0	0

2. A.   Free cash flow to the firm, found with Equation 4-7, is

$$FCFF = NI + NCC + Int(1 - Tax\ rate) - FCInv - WCInv$$
$$FCFF = 285 + 180 + 130(1 - 0.40) - 349 - (39 + 44 - 22 - 23)$$
$$FCFF = 285 + 180 + 78 - 349 - 38 = \$156\ million$$

   B.   Free cash flow to equity, found with Equation 4-10, is

$$FCFE = NI + NCC - FCInv - WCInv + Net\ borrowing$$
$$FCFE = 285 + 180 - 349 - (39 + 44 - 22 - 23) + (10 + 40)$$
$$FCFE = 285 + 180 - 349 - 38 + 50 = \$128\ million$$

C. To find FCFE from FCFF, one uses the relationship in Equation 4-9:

FCFE = FCFF − Int(1 − Tax rate) + Net borrowing
FCFE = 156 − 130(1 − 0.40) + (10 + 40)
FCFE = 156 − 78 + 50 = $128 million

3. A. To find FCFF from CFO, EBIT, or EBITDA, the analyst can use Equations 4-8, 4-12, and 4-13.
    To find FCFF from CFO:

FCFF = CFO + Int(1 − Tax rate) − FCInv
FCFF = 427 + 130(1 − 0.40) − 349 = 427 + 78 − 349 = $156 million

To find FCFF from EBIT:

FCFF = EBIT(1 − Tax rate) + Dep − FCInv − WCInv
FCFF = 605(1 − 0.40) + 180 − 349 − 38
FCFF = 363 + 180 − 349 − 38 = $156 million

Finally, to obtain FCFF from EBITDA:

FCFF = EBITDA(1 − Tax Rate) + Dep(Tax Rate) − FCInv − WCInv
FCFF = 785(1 − 0.40) + 180(0.40) − 349 − 38
FCFF = 471 + 72 − 349 − 38 = $156 million

B. The simplest approach is to calculate FCFF from CFO, EBIT, or EBITDA as was done in part A and then to find FCFE by making the appropriate adjustments to FCFF:

FCFE = FCFF − Int(1 − Tax rate) + Net borrowing.
FCFE = 156 − 130(1 − 0.40) + 50 = 156 − 78 + 50 = $128 million

The analyst can also find FCFE by using CFO, EBIT, or EBITDA directly. Starting with CFO and using Equation 4-11, FCFE is found to be

FCFE = CFO − FCInv + Net borrowing
FCFE = 427 − 349 + 50 = $128 million

Starting with EBIT, on the basis of Equations 4-9 and 4-12, FCFE is

FCFE = EBIT(1 − Tax rate) + Dep − Int(1 − Tax rate) − FCInv − WCInv
       + Net borrowing
FCFE = 605(1 − 0.40) + 180 − 130(1 − 0.40) − 349 − 38 + 50
FCFE = 363 + 180 − 78 − 349 − 38 + 50 = $128 million

Finally, starting with EBITDA, on the basis of Equations 4-9 and 4-13, FCFE is

FCFE = EBITDA(1 − Tax rate) + Dep(Tax rate) − Int(1 − Tax rate) − FCInv
       − WCInv + Net borrowing
FCFE = 785(1 − 0.40) + 180(0.40) − 130(1 − 0.40) − 349 − 38 + 50
FCFE = 471 + 72 − 78 − 349 − 38 + 50 = $128 million

4. A. FCF = Net income + Depreciation and amortization−Cash dividends−Capital expenditures. This definition of free cash flow is sometimes used to determine how much discretionary cash flow management has at its disposal. Management discretion concerning dividends is limited by investor expectations that dividends will be maintained. Comparing this definition with Equation 4-7, FCFF = NI + NCC + Int(1−Tax rate)−FCInv−WCInv, we find that FCFF includes a reduction for investments in working capital and the addition of after-tax interest expense. Common stock dividends are not subtracted from FCFF because dividends represent a distribution of the cash available to investors. (If a company pays preferred dividends and they were previously taken out when net income available to common shareholders was calculated, they are added back in Equation 4-7 to include them in FCFF.)

   B. FCF = Cash flow from operations (from the statement of cash flows)−Capital expenditures. Comparing this definition of free cash flow with Equation 4-8, FCFF = CFO + Int(1−Tax rate)−FCInv, highlights the relationship of CFO to FCFF: The primary point is that when Equation 4-8 is used, after-tax interest is added back to CFO to arrive at the cash flow to all investors. Then FCInv is subtracted to arrive at the amount of that cash flow that is *free* in the sense of available for distribution to those investors after taking care of capital investment needs. If preferred dividends were subtracted to obtain net income (in CFO), they would also have to be added back in. This definition is commonly used to approximate FCFF, but it generally understates the actual FCFF by the amount of after-tax interest expense.

5. A. The firm value is the present value of FCFF discounted at the WACC, or

$$\text{Firm value} = \frac{\text{FCFF}_1}{\text{WACC} - g} = \frac{\text{FCFF}_0(1 + g)}{\text{WACC} - g} = \frac{1.7(1.07)}{0.11 - 0.07} = \frac{1.819}{0.04}$$
$$= \$45.475 \text{ billion}$$

   The market value of equity is the value of the firm minus the value of debt:
   Equity = 45.475−15 = \$30.475 billion

   B. Using the FCFE valuation approach, we find the present value of FCFE discounted at the required rate of return on equity to be

$$\text{PV} = \frac{\text{FCFE}_1}{r - g} = \frac{\text{FCFE}_0(1 + g)}{r - g} = \frac{1.3(1.075)}{0.13 - 0.075} = \frac{1.3975}{0.055} = \$25.409 \text{ billion}$$

   The value of equity using this approach is \$25.409 billion.

6. The required rate of return found with the CAPM is

$$r = E(R_i) = R_F + \beta_i[E(R_M) - R_F] = 6.4\% + 2.1 \ (5.0\%) = 16.9\%$$

The following table shows the values of sales, net income, capital expenditures less depreciation, and investments in working capital. FCFE equals net income less the investments financed with equity:

   FCFE = Net income − (1 − DR)(Capital expenditures − Depreciation)
   − (1 − DR)(Investment in working capital)

where DR is the debt ratio (debt financing as a percentage of debt and equity). Because 20 percent of new investments are financed with debt, 80 percent of the investments are financed with equity, which reduces FCFE by 80 percent of (Capital expenditures − Depreciation) and 80 percent of the investment in working capital.

(All data in billions of Taiwan dollars)	2009	2010	2011	2012	2013
Sales (growing at 28%)	5.500	7.040	9.011	11.534	14.764
Net income = 32% of sales	1.760	2.253	2.884	3.691	4.724
FCInv − Dep = (35%−9%) × Sales	1.430	1.830	2.343	2.999	3.839
WCInv = (6% of Sales)	0.330	0.422	0.541	0.692	0.886
0.80 × (FCInv − Dep + WCInv)	1.408	1.802	2.307	2.953	3.780
FCFE = NI − 0.80 × (FCInv − Dep + WCInv)	0.352	0.451	0.577	0.738	0.945
PV of FCFE discounted at 16.9%	0.301	0.330	0.361	0.395	0.433
Terminal stock value		85.032			
PV of terminal value discounted at 16.9%		38.950			
Total PV of FCFE		1.820			
Total value of firm		40.770			

The terminal stock value is 18.0 times the earnings in 2013, or 18 × 4.724 = $85.03 billion. The present value of the terminal value ($38.95 billion) plus the present value of the first five years' FCFE ($1.82 billion) is $40.77 billion. Because TMI Manufacturing has 17 billion outstanding shares, the value per ordinary share is $2.398.

7. A. The FCFF is (in euro)

$$FCFF = NI + NCC + Int(1 - Tax\ rate) - FCInv - WCInv$$
$$FCFF = 250 + 90 + 150(1 - 0.30) - 170 - 40$$
$$FCFF = 250 + 90 + 105 - 170 - 40 = 235\ million$$

The weighted-average cost of capital is

$$WACC = 9\%(1 - 0.30)(0.40) + 13\%(0.60) = 10.32\%$$

The value of the firm (in euro) is

$$Firm\ value = \frac{FCFF_1}{WACC - g} = \frac{FCFF_0(1 + g)}{WACC - g} = \frac{235(1.06)}{0.1032 - 0.06} = \frac{249.1}{0.0432}$$
$$= 5,766.20\ million$$

The total value of equity is the total firm value minus the value of debt, Equity = €5,766.20 million − €1,800 million = €3,966.20 million. Dividing by the number of shares gives the per-share estimate of V_0 = €3,966.20 million/10 million = €396.62 per share.

B. The free cash flow to equity is

$$FCFE = NI + NCC - FCInv - WCInv + Net\ borrowing$$
$$FCFE = 250 + 90 - 170 - 40 + 0.40(170 - 90 + 40)$$
$$FCFE = 250 + 90 - 170 - 40 + 48 = €178\ million$$

Because the company is borrowing 40 percent of the increase in net capital expenditures (170 − 90) and working capital (40), net borrowing is €48 million.

The total value of equity is the FCFE discounted at the required rate of return of equity:

$$\text{Equity value} = \frac{\text{FCFE}_1}{r-g} = \frac{\text{FCFE}_0(1+g)}{r-g} = \frac{178(1.07)}{0.13-0.07} = \frac{190.46}{0.06} = €3{,}174.33 \text{ million}$$

The value per share is V_0 = €3,174.33 million/10 million = €317.43 per share.

8. The WACC for PHB Company is

$$\text{WACC} = 0.30(7.0\%)(1-0.35) + 0.15(6.8\%) + 0.55(11.0\%) = 8.435\%$$

The firm value is

Firm value = FCFF$_0$(1 + g)/(WACC – g)

Firm value = 28(1.04)/(0.08435 − 0.04) = 29.12/0.04435 = $656.60 million

The value of equity is the firm value minus the value of debt minus the value of preferred stock: Equity = 656.60 − 145 − 65 = $446.60 million. Dividing this amount by the number of shares gives the estimated value per share of $446.60 million/8 million shares = $55.82.

The estimated value for the stock is greater than the market price of $32.50, so the stock appears to be undervalued.

9. A. The required return on equity is

$$r = E(R_i) = R_F + \beta_i[E(R_M) - R_F] = 5.5\% + 0.90(5.5\%) = 10.45\%$$

The weighted-average cost of capital is

$$\text{WACC} = 0.25(7.0\%)(1-0.40) + 0.75(10.45\%) = 8.89\%$$

B. Firm value $= \dfrac{\text{FCFF}_0(1+g)}{\text{WACC} - g}$

Firm value $= \dfrac{1.1559(1.04)}{0.0889 - 0.04} = \$24.583$

C. Equity value = Firm value − Market value of debt
   Equity value = 24.583 − 3.192 = $21.391 billion

D. Value per share = Equity value/Number of shares
   Value per share = $21.391 billion/1.852 billion = $11.55

10. A. The required rate of return for McInish found with the CAPM is

$$r = E(R_i) = R_F + \beta_i[E(R_M) - R_F] = 5.08\% + 0.70(5.50\%) = 8.93\%$$

The value per share is

$$V_0 = \frac{\text{FCFE}_0(1+g)}{r-g} = \frac{0.88(1.064)}{0.0893 - 0.064} = \$37.01$$

B. The following table shows the calculated price for McInish based on the base-case values for all values except the variable being changed from the base-case value.

Variable	Estimated Price with Low Value	Estimated Price with High Value	Range (Rank)
Normalized $FCFE_0$	$29.44	$47.94	$18.50 (3)
Risk-free rate	$38.22	$35.33	$ 2.89 (5)
Equity risk premium	$51.17	$28.99	$22.18 (2)
Beta	$47.29	$30.40	$16.89 (4)
FCFE growth rate	$18.56	$48.79	$30.23 (1)

As the table shows, the value of McInish is most sensitive to the changes in the FCFE growth rate, with the price moving over a wide range. McInish's stock price is least sensitive to alternative values of the risk-free rate. Alternative values of beta, the equity risk premium, or the initial FCFE value also have a large impact on the value of the stock, although the effects of these variables are smaller than the effect of the growth rate.

11. A. Using the CAPM, the required rate of return for NewMarket is

$$r = E(R_i) = R_F + \beta_i[E(R_M) - R_F] = 7\% + 1.3(4\%) = 12.2\%$$

To estimate FCFE, we use Equation 4-15:

$$FCFE = \text{Net income} - (1 - DR)(FCInv - Depreciation) - (1 - DR)(WCInv)$$

which can be written

$$FCFE = \text{Net income} - (1 - DR)(FCInv - Depreciation + WCInv)$$
$$= \text{Net income} - (1 - DR)(\text{Net investment in operating assets})$$

The following table shows that net income grows at 20 percent annually for years 1, 2, and 3 and then grows at 8 percent for year 4. The net investment in operating assets is $1,150 million in year 1 and grows at 15 percent annually for years 2 and 3. Debt financing is 40 percent of this investment. FCFE is NI−Net investment in operating assets + New debt financing. Finally, the present value of FCFE for years 1, 2, and 3 is found by discounting at 12.2 percent.

(in $ millions)	Year			
	1	2	3	4
Net income	720.00	864.00	1,036.80	1,119.74
Net investment in operating assets	1,150.00	1,322.50	1,520.88	335.92
New debt financing	460.00	529.00	608.35	134.37
FCFE	30.00	70.50	124.27	918.19
PV of FCFE discounted at 12.2%	26.74	56.00	87.98	

In year 4, net income is 8 percent larger than in year 3. In year 4, the investment in operating assets is 30 percent of net income and debt financing is 40 percent of this investment. The FCFE in year 4 is $918.19 million. The value of FCFE after year 3 is found by using the constant-growth model:

$$V_3 = \frac{FCFE_4}{r - g} = \frac{918.19}{0.122 - 0.08} = \$21,861.67 \text{ million}$$

The present value of V_3 discounted at 12.2 percent is $15,477.64 million. The total value of equity, the present value of the first three years' FCFE plus the present value of V_3, is $15,648.36 million. Dividing this by the number of outstanding shares (318 million) gives a value per share of $49.21. For the first three years, NewMarket has a small FCFE because of the large investments it is making during the high-growth phase. In the normal-growth phase, FCFE is much larger because the investments required are much smaller.

B. The planner's estimate of the share value of $70.98 is much higher than the FCFE model estimate of $49.21 for several reasons. First, taxes and interest expenses have a prior claim to the company's cash flow and should be taken out of the cash flows used in estimating the value of equity because these amounts are not available to equity holders. The planner did not do this.

Second, EBITDA does not account for the company's reinvestments in operating assets. So EBITDA overstates the funds available to stockholders if reinvestment needs exceed depreciation charges, which is the case for growing companies such as NewMarket.

Third, EBITDA does not account for the company's capital structure. Using EBITDA to represent a benefit to stockholders (as opposed to stockholders and bondholders combined) is a mistake.

Finally, dividing EBITDA by the bond rate commits a major error. The risk-free bond rate is an inappropriate discount rate for risky equity cash flows; the proper measure is the required rate of return on the company's equity. Dividing by a fixed rate also assumes, erroneously, that the cash flow stream is a fixed perpetuity. EBITDA cannot be a perpetual stream because if it were distributed, the stream would eventually decline to zero (lacking capital investments). NewMarket is actually a growing company, so assuming it to be a nongrowing perpetuity is a mistake.

12. The following table develops the information to calculate FCFE per share (amounts are in U.S. dollars).

	2003	2004	2005	2006	2007	2008
Growth rate for EPS	21%	18%	15%	12%	9%	6%
EPS	3.630	4.283	4.926	5.517	6.014	6.374
Capital expenditure per share	5.000	5.000	4.500	4.000	3.500	1.500
Investment in WC per share	1.250	1.250	1.125	1.000	0.875	0.375
New debt financing = 40% of (Capital expenditure + WCInv)	2.500	2.500	2.250	2.000	1.750	0.750
FCFE = NI − Capital expenditure − WCInv + New debt financing	−0.120	0.533	1.551	2.517	3.389	5.249
PV of FCFE discounted at 12%	−0.107	0.425	1.104	1.600	1.923	

Earnings per share for 2002 are $3.00, and the EPS estimates for 2003 through 2008 in the table are found by increasing the previous year's EPS by that year's growth rate. The net capital expenditures each year were specified by the analyst. The increase in working capital per share is equal to 25 percent of net capital expenditures. Finally, debt financing is 40 percent of that year's total net capital expenditures and investment in working capital. For example, in 2003, the per-share amount for net capital expenditures plus investment in working capital is $5.00 + $1.25 = $6.25. Debt financing is 40 percent of $6.25, or $2.50. Debt financing for 2004 through 2008 is found in the same way.

FCFE equals net income minus net capital expenditures minus investment in working capital plus new debt financing. Notice that FCFE is negative in 2003 because of large capital investments and investments in working capital. As these investments decline relative to net income, FCFE becomes positive and substantial.

The present values of FCFE from 2003 through 2007 are given in the bottom row of the table. These five present values sum to $4.944 per share. Because FCFE from 2008 onward will grow at a constant 6 percent, the constant-growth model can be used to value these cash flows:

$$V_{2007} = \frac{FCFE_{2008}}{r - g} = \frac{5.249}{0.12 - 0.06} = \$87.483$$

The present value of this stream is $87.483/(1.12)^5 = \$49.640$. The value per share is the present value of the first five FCFEs (2003 through 2007) plus the present value of the FCFE after 2007, or $4.944 + \$49.640 = \$54.58$.

13. A. FCFE is defined as the cash flow remaining after the company meets all financial obligations, including debt payment, and covers all capital expenditure and working capital needs. Sundanci's FCFE for the year 2008 is calculated as follows:

Net income	$80 million
Plus: Depreciation expense	23
Less: Capital expenditures	38
Less: Investment in WC	41
Equals: FCFE	$24 million

Thus, FCFE per share equals ($24 million)/(84 million shares) = $0.286.

B. The FCFE model requires forecasts of FCFE for the high-growth years (2009 and 2010) plus a forecast for the first year of stable growth (2011) to allow for an estimate of the terminal value in 2010 based on constant perpetual growth. Because all of the components of FCFE are expected to grow at the same rate, the values can be obtained by projecting the FCFE at the common rate. (Alternatively, the components of FCFE can be projected and aggregated for each year.)

The following table provides the process for estimating Sundanci's current value on a per-share basis.

Free Cash Flow to Equity					
Base assumptions:					
Shares outstanding (millions)	84				
Required return on equity, *r*	14%				
		Actual 2008	Projected 2009	Projected 2010	Projected 2011
	Total	Per share	*g* = 27%	*g* = 27%	*g* = 13%
Earnings after tax	$80	$0.952	$1.2090	$1.5355	$1.7351
Plus: Depreciation expense	$23	$0.274	$0.3480	$0.4419	$0.4994
Less: Capital expenditures	$38	$0.452	$0.5740	$0.7290	$0.8238
Less: Increase in net working capital	$41	$0.488	$0.6198	$0.7871	$0.8894
Equals: FCFE	$24	$0.286	$0.3632	$0.4613	$0.5213
Terminal value[a]				$52.1300	
Total cash flows to equity[b]			$0.3632	$52.5913	
Discounted value[c]			$0.3186	$40.4673	
Current value per share[d]	$40.7859				

[a]Projected 2010 terminal value = Projected 2011 FCFE/$(r - g)$.
[b]Projected 2010 total cash flows to equity = Projected 2010 FCFE + Projected 2010 terminal value.
[c]Discounted values obtained by using r = 14 percent.
[d]Current value per share = Discounted value 2009 + Discounted value 2010.

C. The following limitations of the DDM *are* addressed by the FCFE model: The DDM uses a strict definition of cash flow to equity; that is, cash flows to equity are the dividends on the common stock. The FCFE model expands the definition of cash flow to include the balance of residual cash flows after all financial obligations and investment needs have been met. Thus, the FCFE model explicitly recognizes the company's investment and financing policies as well as its dividend policy. In instances of a change of corporate control, and thus the possibility of changing dividend policy, the FCFE model provides a better estimate of value.

Both two-stage valuation models allow for two distinct phases of growth—an initial finite period when the growth is abnormal followed by a stable growth period that is expected to last forever. These two-stage models share the same three limitations with respect to the growth assumptions:

   i. The analyst must confront the difficulty of defining the duration of the extraordinary growth period. A long period of high growth will produce a higher valuation, and the analyst may be tempted to assume an unrealistically long period of extraordinary growth.
   ii. The analyst must realize that assuming a sudden shift from high growth to lower, stable growth is unrealistic. The transformation is more likely to occur gradually over time.

iii. Because value is quite sensitive to the steady-state growth assumption, overestimating or underestimating this rate can lead to large errors in value.

The two models also share other limitations—notably, difficulties in accurately estimating required rates of return.

14. A. When a two-stage DDM is used, the value of a share of Mackinac, using dividends per share (DPS), is calculated as follows:

$$DPS_0 = \text{Cash dividends/Shares outstanding} = \$22,470/13,000 = \$1.7285$$
$$DPS_1 = DPS_0 \times 1.17 = \$2.0223$$
$$DPS_2 = DPS_0 \times 1.17^2 = \$2.3661$$
$$DPS_3 = DPS_0 \times 1.17^3 = \$2.7683$$
$$DPS_4 = DPS_0 \times 1.17^3 \times 1.09 = \$3.0175$$

When the CAPM is used, the required return on equity, r, is

$$r = \text{Government bond rate} + (\text{Beta} \times \text{Equity risk premium})$$
$$= 0.06 + (1.25 \times 0.05) = 0.1225 \text{ or } 12.25 \text{ percent}$$

$$\text{Value per share} = DPS_1/(1 + r) + DPS_2/(1 + r)^2 + DPS_3/(1 + r)^3$$
$$+ [DPS_4/(r - g_{stable})]/(1 + r)^3$$

$$\text{Value per share} = \$2.0223/1.1225 + \$2.3661/1.1225^2 + \$2.7683/1.1225^3$$
$$+ [\$3.0175/(0.1225 - 0.09)]/1.1225^3$$
$$= \$1.8016 + \$1.8778 + \$1.9573 + \$65.6450 = \$71.28$$

B. When the two-stage FCFE model is used, the value of a share of Mackinac is calculated as follows (in $ thousands, except per-share data):

Net income = \$37,450
Depreciation = \$10,500
Capital expenditures = \$15,000
Change in working capital = \$5,500
New debt issuance − Principal repayments = Change in debt outstanding = \$4,000
$FCFE_0$ = Net income + Depreciation − Capital expenditures
   − Change in working Capital − Principal repayments + New debt issues
$FCFE_0$ = \$37,450 + \$10,500 − \$15,000 − \$5,500 + \$4,000 = \$31,450
$FCFE_0$ per share = \$31,450/13,000 = \$2.4192
$FCFE_1 = FCFE_0 \times 1.17 = \$2.8305$
$FCFE_2 = FCFE_0 \times 1.17^2 = \$3.3117$
$FCFE_3 = FCFE_0 \times 1.17^3 = \$3.8747$
$FCFE_4 = FCFE_0 \times 1.17^3 \times 1.09 = \$4.2234$

From the answer to A, $r = 12.25$ percent.

$$\text{Value per share} = FCFE_1/(1 + r) + FCFE_2/(1 + r)^2 + FCFE_3/(1 + r)^3$$
$$+ [FCFE_4/(r - g_{stable})]/(1 + r)^3$$
$$\text{Value per share} = \$2.8305/1.1225 + \$3.3117/1.1225^2 + \$3.8747/1.1225^3$$
$$+ [\$4.2234/(0.1225 - 0.09)]/1.1225^3$$
$$= \$2.5216 + \$2.6283 + \$2.7395 + \$91.8798 = \$99.77$$

C. The FCFE model is best for valuing companies for takeovers or in situations that have a reasonable chance of a change in corporate control. Because controlling stockholders can change the dividend policy, they are interested in estimating the maximum residual cash flow after meeting all financial obligations and investment needs. The DDM is based on the premise that the only cash flows received by stockholders are dividends. FCFE uses a more expansive definition to measure what a company can afford to pay out as dividends.

15. A. The real required rate of return for SK Telecom is

Country return (real)	6.50%
Industry adjustment	+0.60%
Size adjustment	−0.10%
Leverage adjustment	+0.25%
Required rate of return	7.25%

B. The real growth rate of FCFE is expected to be the same as the country rate of 3.5 percent. The value of one share is

$$V_0 = \frac{FCFE_0(1 + g_{real})}{r_{real} - g_{real}} = \frac{1,300(1.035)}{0.0725 - 0.035} = 35,880 \text{ Korean won}$$

16. The required return for QuickChange, found by using the CAPM, is $r = E(R_i) = R_F + \beta_i[E(R_M) - R_F] = 4.5\% + 2.0(5.0\%) = 14.5\%$. The estimated future values of FCFE are given in the following exhibit (amounts in U.S. dollars):

Year t	Variable	Calculation	Value in Year t	Present Value at 14.5%
1	$FCFE_1$	0.75(1.10)	0.825	0.721
2	$FCFE_2$	0.75(1.10)(1.26)	1.040	0.793
3	$FCFE_3$	0.75(1.10)(1.26)^2	1.310	0.873
4	$FCFE_4$	0.75(1.10)(1.26)^3	1.650	0.960
4	TV_4	$FCFE_5/(r-g)$	20.580	11.974
		$= 0.75(1.10)(1.26)^3(1.06)/(0.145 - 0.06)$		
		$= 1.749/0.085$		
0		Total value = PV of FCFE for years 1–4		15.32
		+ PV of Terminal value		

The FCFE grows at 10 percent for year 1 and then at 26 percent for years 2–4. These calculated values for FCFE are shown in the exhibit. The present values of the FCFE for the first four years discounted at the required rate of return are given in the last column of the table. After year 4, FCFE will grow at 6 percent forever, so the constant-growth FCFE model is used to find the terminal value at time 4, which is $TV_4 = FCFE_5/(r - g)$. TV_4 is discounted at the required return for four periods to find its present value, as shown in the table. Finally, the total value of the stock, $15.32, is the sum of the present values of the first four years' FCFE per share plus the present value of the terminal value per share.

17. The total value of nonoperating assets is

> $60 million short-term securities
> $45 million market value of noncurrent assets
> $40 million pension fund surplus
> _____
> $145 million nonoperating assets

The total value of the firm is the value of the operating assets plus the value of the non-operating assets, or $720 million plus $145 million = $865 million. The equity value is the value of the firm minus the value of debt, or $865 million−$215 million = $650 million. The value per share is $650 million/100 million shares = $6.50 per share.

18. C is correct. The sustainable growth rate is return on equity (ROE) multiplied by the retention ratio. ROE is 10 percent, and the retention ratio is 1−Payout ratio, or 1.0−0.2 = 0.8. The sustainable growth rate is 0.8 × 10% = 8%. Because Emerald's policy states that dividend growth will not exceed FCFE growth, FCFE growth should be at least 8 percent per year in the long term.

19. A is correct. Justifications for choosing the FCFE model over the DDM include:
    - The company pays dividends but its dividends differ significantly from the company's capacity to pay dividends (the first reason given by Leigh).
    - The investor takes a control perspective (the second reason given by Leigh).

20. A is correct. FCFF = NI + NCC + Interest expense (1 − Tax rate) − FCInv − WCInv. In this case:

    NI = $485 million
    NCC = Depreciation expense = $270 million
    Interest expense (1 − Tax rate) = 195 (1 − 0.32) = $132.6 million
    FCInv = Netpurchase of fixed assets = Increase in gross fixed assets
       = 4,275 − 3,752 = $523 million
    WCInv = Increase in accounts receivable + Increase in inventory
          − Increase in accounts payable − Increase in accrued liabilities = (770 − 711)
          + (846 − 780) − (476 − 443) − (149 − 114) = $57 million
    FCFF = 485 + 270 + 132.6−523−57 = 307.6, or $308 million

21. B is correct. FCFE = NI + NCC−FCInv−WCInv + Net borrowing. In this case:

    NI = $485 million
    NCC = Depreciation expense = $270 million
    FCInv = Net purchase of fixed assets = Increase in gross fixed assets
       = 4,275 − 3,752 = $523 million
    WCInv = Increase in accounts receivable + Increase in inventory
          − Increase in accounts payable − Increase in accrued liabilities
          = (770 − 711) + (846 − 780) − (476 − 443) − (149 − 114) = $57 million
    Net borrowing = Increase in notes payable + Increase in long-term debt = (465
          − 450) + (1,575 − 1,515) = $75 million
    FCFE = 485 + 270 − 523 − 57 + 75 = $250 million

An alternative calculation is

    FCFE = FCFF − Int(1 − Tax rate) + Net borrowing
    FCFE = 307.6 − 195 (1 − 0.32) + (15 + 60) = $250 million

22. C is correct. Inventory cannot be reduced below zero. Furthermore, sales growth tends to increase inventory.

23. A is correct. The FCFF model is often selected when the capital structure is expected to change because FCFF estimation may be easier than FCFE estimation in the presence of changing financial leverage.

CHAPTER 5

RESIDUAL INCOME VALUATION

SOLUTIONS

1. Yes, VIM earned a positive residual income of $8,000.

EBIT	$ 300,000	
Interest	120,000	($2,000,000 × 6%)
Pretax income	$ 180,000	
Tax expense	72,000	
Net income	$ 108,000	

Equity charge = Equity capital × Required return on equity

$\quad$ = (1/3)($3,000,000) × 0.10

$\quad$ = $1,000,000 × 0.10 = $100,000

Residual income = Net income − Equity charge

$\quad$ = $108,000 – $100,000 = $8,000

2. According to the residual income model, the intrinsic value of a share of common stock equals book value per share plus the present value of expected future per-share residual income. Book value per share was given as $20. Noting that debt is $2,000,000 [(2/3)($3,000,000)] so that interest is $120,000 ($2,000,000 × 6%), VIM's residual income is $8,000, which is calculated (as in problem 1) as follows:

Residual income = Net income – Equity charge

$\quad$ = [(EBIT – Interest)(1 – Tax rate)]

$\qquad$ – [(Equity capital)(Required return on equity)]

$\quad$ = [($300,000 – $120,000)(1 – 0.40)] – [($1,000,000)(0.10)]

$\quad$ = $108,000 – $100,000

$\quad$ = $8,000

Therefore, residual income per share is $0.16 per share ($8,000/50,000 shares). Because EBIT is expected to continue at the current level indefinitely, the expected per-share residual income of $0.16 is treated as a perpetuity. The present value of $0.16 is discounted at the required return on equity of 10 percent, so the present value of the residual income is $1.60 ($0.16/0.10).

$$\text{Intrinsic value} = \text{Book value per share} + \text{PV of expected future per-share residual income}$$
$$= \$20 + \$1.60 = \$21.60$$

3. With $g = b \times \text{ROE} = (1 - 0.80)(0.15) = (0.20)(0.15) = 0.03,$

$$P/B = (\text{ROE} - g)/(r - g)$$
$$= (0.15 - 0.03)/(0.12 - 0.03)$$
$$= 0.12/0.09 = 1.33$$

or

$$P/B = 1 + (\text{ROE} - r)/(r - g)$$
$$= 1 + (0.15 - 0.12)/(0.12 - 0.03)$$
$$= 1.33$$

4. In this problem (unlike problems 1 and 2), interest expense has already been deducted in arriving at NMP's pretax income of $5.1 million. Therefore,

$$\text{Net income} = \text{Pretax income} \times (1 - \text{Tax rate})$$
$$= \$5.1 \text{ million} \times (1 - 0.4)$$
$$= \$5.1 \times 0.6 = \$3.06 \text{ million}$$
$$\text{Equity charge} = \text{Total equity} \times \text{Cost of equity capital}$$
$$= (0.1 \times \$450 \text{ million}) \times 12\%$$
$$= \$45 \text{ million} \times 0.12 = \$5,400,000$$
$$\text{Residual income} = \text{Net income} - \text{Equity charge}$$
$$= \$3,060,000 - \$5,400,000 = -\$2,340,000$$

NMP had negative residual income of $-\$2,340,000$.

5. To achieve a positive residual income, a company's net operating profit after taxes as a percentage of its total assets can be compared with its weighted average cost of capital (WACC). For SWI,

$$\text{NOPAT/Assets} = \text{\euro}10 \text{ million}/\text{\euro}100 \text{million} = 10\%$$
$$\text{WACC} = (\text{Percent of debt} \times \text{After-tax cost of debt}) + (\text{Percent of equity} \times \text{Cost of equity})$$
$$= (0.5)(0.09)(0.6) + (0.5)(0.12)$$
$$= (0.5)(0.054) + (0.5)(0.12) = 0.027 + 0.06 = 0.087 = 8.7\%$$

Therefore, SWI's residual income was positive. Specifically, residual income equals €1.3 million [$(0.10 - 0.087) \times \text{\euro}100$ million].

6. A. $\text{EVA} = \text{NOPAT} - \text{WACC} \times \text{Beginning book value of assets}$
$$= \$100 - (11\%) \times (\$200 + \$300) = \$100 - (11\%)(\$500) = \$45$$

    B. RI_t = $E_t - rB_{t-1}$
               = €5.00 − (11%)(€30.00) = €5.00 − €3.30 = €1.70
    C. RI_t = $(\text{ROE}_t - r) \times B_{t-1}$
               = (18% − 12%) × (€30) = €1.80

7. A. Economic value added = Net operating profit after taxes − (Cost of capital × Total capital) = $100 million − (14% × $700 million) = $2 million. In the absence of information that would be required to calculate the weighted average cost of debt and equity, and given that Sundanci has no long-term debt, the only capital cost used is the required rate of return on equity of 14 percent.
   B. Market value added = Market value of capital − Total capital
   $26 stock price × 84 million shares − $700 million = $1.48 billion

8. A. Because the dividend is a perpetuity, the no-growth form of the DDM is applied as follows:

$$V_0 = D/r$$
$$= \$0.60/0.12 = \$5 \text{ per share}$$

   B. According to the residual income model, V_0 = Book value per share + Present value of expected future per-share residual income.
   Residual income is calculated as:

$$\text{RI}_t = E - rB_{t-1}$$
$$= \$0.60 - (0.12)(\$6) = -\$0.12$$

Present value of perpetual stream of residual income is calculated as:

$$\text{RI}_t/r = -\$0.12/0.12 = -\$1.00$$

The value is calculated as:

$$V_0 = \$6.00 - \$1.00 = \$5.00 \text{ per share}$$

9. A. According to the DDM, $V_0 = D/r$ for a no-growth company.

$$V_0 = \$2.00/0.125 = \$16 \text{ per share}$$

   B. Under the residual income model, $V_0 = B_0$ + Present value of expected future per-share residual income.
   Residual income is calculated as:

$$\text{RI}_t = E - rB_{t-1}$$
$$= \$2 - (0.125)(\$10) = \$0.75$$

Present value of stream of residual income is calculated as:

$$\text{RI}_t/r = 0.75/0.125 = \$6$$

The value is calculated as:

$$V_0 = \$10 + \$6 = \$16 \text{ per share}$$

10. A. V_0 = Present value of the future dividends
    = $2/1.10 + \$2.50/(1.1)^2 + \$20.50/(1.1)^3$
    = $1.818 + \$2.066 + \$15.402 = \$19.286$

    B. The book values and residual incomes for the next three years are as follows:

Year	1	2	3
Beginning book value	$ 8.00	$10.00	$ 12.50
Retained earnings (Net income – Dividends)	2.00	2.50	(12.50)
Ending book value	$10.00	$12.50	$ 0.00
Net income	$ 4.00	$ 5.00	$ 8.00
Less equity charge ($r \times$ Book value)	0.80	1.00	1.25
Residual income	$ 3.20	$ 4.00	$ 6.75

Under the residual income model,

$V_0 = B_0 +$ Present value of expected future per-share residual income

$V_0 = \$8.00 + \$3.20/1.1 + \$4.00/(1.1)^2 + \$6.75/(1.1)^3$

$V_0 = \$8.00 + \$2.909 + \$3.306 + \$5.071 = \$19.286$

C.

Year	1	2	3
Net income (NI)	$4.00	$5.00	$8.00
Beginning book value (BV)	8.00	10.00	12.50
Return on equity (ROE) = NI/BV	50%	50%	64%
ROE $- r$	40%	40%	54%
Residual income (ROE $- r$) $\times$ BV	$3.20	$4.00	$6.75

Under the residual income model,

$V_0 = B_0 +$ Present value of expected future per-share residual income

$V_0 = \$8.00 + \$3.20/1.1 + \$4.00/(1.1)^2 + \$6.75/(1.1)^3$

$V_0 = \$8.00 + \$2.909 + \$3.306 + \$5.071 = \$19.286$

Note: Because the residual incomes for each year are necessarily the same in parts B and C, the results for stock valuation are identical.

11.

Year	2008	2009	2012
Beginning book value	$30.00	$33.00	$43.92
Net income = ROE $\times$ Book value	4.50	4.95	6.59
Dividends = payout $\times$ Net income	1.50	1.65	2.20
Equity charge ($r \times$ Book value)	3.60	3.96	5.27
Residual income = Net income $-$ Equity charge	0.90	0.99	1.32
Ending book value	$33.00	$36.30	$48.32

The table shows that residual income in 2008 is $0.90, which equals Beginning book value $\times$ (ROE $- r$) = $30 $\times$ (0.15 $-$ 0.12). The 2009 column shows that residual income grew by 10 percent to $0.99, which follows from the fact that growth in residual income relates directly to the growth in net income as this example is configured. When both net income and dividends are a function of book value and return on equity is constant, then growth, g, can be predicted from (ROE)(1 − Dividend payout ratio). In this case, $g = 0.15 \times (1 − 0.333) = 0.10$ or 10 percent. Net income and residual income will grow by 10 percent annually.

Therefore, residual income in year 2012 = (Residual income in year 2008) $\times (1.1)^4 = 0.90 \times 1.4641 = \$1.32$.

12. When such items as changes in the value of available-for-sale securities bypass the income statement, they are generally assumed to be nonoperating items that will fluctuate from year to year, although averaging to zero in a period of years. The evidence suggests, however, that changes in the value of available-for-sale securities are not averaging to zero but are persistently negative. Furthermore, these losses are bypassing the income statement. It appears that the company is either making an inaccurate assumption or misleading investors in one way or another. Accordingly, Kent might adjust LE's income downward by the amount of loss for other comprehensive income for each of those years. ROE would then decline commensurately. LE's book value would *not* be misstated because the decline in the value of these securities was already recognized and appears in the shareholders' equity account as "Accumulated Other Comprehensive Income."

13. $V_0 = B_0 + (\text{ROE} − r)B_0/(r − g)$
    $= \$20 + (0.18 − 0.14)(\$20)/(0.14 − 0.10)$
    $= \$20 + \$20 = \$40$

Given that the current market price is \$35 and the estimated value is \$40, Simms will probably conclude that the shares are somewhat undervalued.

14. $V_0 = B_0 + (\text{ROE} − r)B_0/(r − g)$
    $= \$30 + (0.15 − 0.12)(\$30)/(0.12 − 0.10)$
    $= \$30 + \$45 = \$75$ per share

15.

Year	Net Income (Projected)	Ending Book Value	ROE (%)	Equity Charge (in currency)	Residual Income	PV of RI
2007		\$10.00				
2008	\$1.50	11.50	15	\$1.00	\$0.50	\$0.45
2009	1.73	13.23	15	1.15	0.58	0.48
2010	1.99	15.22	15	1.32	0.67	0.50
2011	2.29	17.51	15	1.52	0.77	0.53
2012	2.63	20.14	15	1.75	0.88	0.55
						\$2.51

Using the finite horizon form of residual income valuation,

$V_0 = B_0 +$ Sum of discounted RIs + Premium (also discounted to present)
    $= \$10 + \$2.51 + (0.20)(20.14)/(1.10)^5$
    $= \$10 + \$2.51 + \$2.50 = \$15.01$

16. A. Columns (a) through (d) in the table show calculations for beginning book value, net income, dividends, and ending book value.

Year	(a) Beginning Book Value	(b) Net Income	(c) Dividends	(d) Ending Book Value	(e) Residual Income	(f) PV of RI
1	$9.620	$2.116	$0.635	$11.101	$1.318	$1.217
2	11.101	2.442	0.733	12.811	1.521	1.297
3	12.811	2.818	0.846	14.784	1.755	1.382
4	14.784	3.252	0.976	17.061	2.025	1.472
5	17.061	3.753	1.126	19.688	2.337	1.569
6	19.688	4.331	1.299	22.720	2.697	1.672
7	22.720	4.998	1.500	26.219	3.113	1.781
8	26.219	5.768	1.730	30.257	3.592	1.898
Total						$12.288

For each year, net income is 22 percent of beginning book value. Dividends are 30 percent of net income. The ending book value equals the beginning book value plus net income minus dividends.

B. Column (e) shows residual income, which equals Net income – Cost of equity (%) × Beginning book value.

To find the cost of equity, use the CAPM:

$$r = R_F + \beta_i [E(R_M) - R_F] = 5\% + (0.60)(5.5\%) = 8.30\%$$

For year 1 in the table,

$$\text{Residual income} = RI_t = E - rB_{t-1}$$
$$= 2.116 - (8.30\%)(9.62)$$
$$= 2.116 - 0.798 = \$1.318$$

This same calculation is repeated for years 2 through 8.

The final column of the table, (f), gives the present value of the calculated residual income, discounted at 8.30 percent.

C. To find the stock value with the residual income method, use this equation:

$$V_0 = B_0 + \sum_{t=1}^{T} \frac{(E_t - rB_{t-1})}{(1 + r)^t} + \frac{P_T - B_T}{(1 + r)^T}$$

- In this equation, B_0 is the current book value per share of $9.62.
- The second term, the sum of the present values of the eight years' residual income, is shown in the table: $12.288.
- To estimate the final term, the present value of the excess of the terminal stock price over the terminal book value, use the assumption that the terminal stock price is assumed to be 3.0 times the terminal book value. So, by assumption, the terminal stock price is $90.771 [$P_T = 3.0(30.257)$]. $P_T - B_T$ is $60.514 (90.771 – 30.257), and the present value of this amount discounted at 8.30 percent for eight years is $31.976.
- Summing the relevant terms gives a stock price of $53.884 ($V_0 = 9.62 + 12.288 + 31.976$).

D. The appropriate DDM expression expresses the value of the stock as the sum of the present value of the dividends plus the present value of the terminal value:

$$V_0 = \sum_{t=1}^{T} \frac{D_t}{(1+r)^t} + \frac{P_T}{(1+r)^T}$$

Discounting the dividends from the table shown in the solution to part A at 8.30 percent gives:

Year	Dividend	PV of Dividend
1	$0.635	$0.586
2	0.733	0.625
3	0.846	0.666
4	0.976	0.709
5	1.126	0.756
6	1.299	0.805
7	1.500	0.858
8	1.730	0.914
All		$5.919

- The present value of the eight dividends is $5.92. The estimated terminal stock price, calculated in the solution to part C, is $90.771, which equals $47.964 discounted at 8.30 percent for eight years.
- The value for the stock, the present value of the dividends plus the present value of the terminal stock price, is $V_0 = 5.92 + 47.964 = \$53.884$.
- The stock values estimated with the residual income model and the dividend discount model are identical. Because they are based on similar financial assumptions, this equivalency is expected. Even though the two models differ in their timing of the recognition of value, their final results are the same.

17. A. The justified P/B can be found with the following formula:

$$\frac{P_0}{B_0} = 1 + \frac{ROE - r}{r - g}$$

ROE is 20 percent, g is 6 percent, and r is 9.4% $[R_F + \beta_i[E(R_M) - R_F] = 5\% + (0.80)(5.5\%)]$. Substituting in the values gives a justified P/B of

$$\frac{P_0}{B_0} = 1 + \frac{0.20 - 0.094}{0.094 - 0.06} = 4.12$$

The assumed parameters give a justified P/B of 4.12, slightly above the current P/B of 3.57.

B.   To find the ROE that would result in a P/B of 3.57, we substitute 3.57, r, and g into the following equation:

$$\frac{P_0}{B_0} = 1 + \frac{ROE - r}{r - g}$$

This yields

$$3.57 = 1 + \frac{ROE - 0.094}{0.094 - 0.06}$$

Solving for ROE requires several steps to finally derive an ROE of 0.18138 or 18.1 percent. This value of ROE is consistent with a P/B of 3.57.

C.   To find the growth rate that would result with a P/B of 3.57, use the expression given in part B, but solve for g instead of ROE:

$$\frac{P_0}{B_0} = 1 + \frac{ROE - r}{r - g}$$

Substituting in the values gives:

$$3.57 = 1 + \frac{0.20 - 0.094}{0.094 - g}$$

The growth rate g is 0.05275 or 5.3 percent. Assuming that the single-stage growth model is applicable to Boeing, the current P/B and current market price can be justified with values for ROE or g that are not much different from the starting values of 20 percent and 6 percent, respectively.

CHAPTER 6

MARKET-BASED VALUATION: PRICE AND ENTERPRISE VALUE MULTIPLES

SOLUTIONS

1. A. Normalized EPS is the level of earnings per share that the company could currently achieve under midcyclical conditions.

   B. Averaging EPS over the 2003–2006 period, we find that ($2.55 + $2.13 + $0.23 + $1.45)/4 = $1.59. According to the method of historical average EPS, Jonash's normalized EPS is $1.59. The P/E based on this estimate is $57.98/1.59 = 36.5.

   C. Averaging ROE over the 2003–2006 period, we find that (0.218 + 0.163 + 0.016 + 0.089)/4 = 0.1215. For current BV per share, you would use the estimated value of $19.20 for year-end 2007. According to the method of average ROE, 0.1215 × $19.20 = $2.33 is the normalized EPS. The P/E based on this estimate is $57.98/$2.33 = 24.9.

2. A. The analyst can rank the two stocks by earnings yield (E/P). Whether EPS is positive or negative, a lower E/P reflects a richer (higher) valuation and a ranking from high to low E/P has a meaningful interpretation.

   In some cases, an analyst might handle negative EPS by using normalized EPS in its place. Neither business, however, has a history of profitability. When year-ahead EPS is expected to be positive, forward P/E is positive. Thus, the use of forward P/Es sometimes addresses the problem of trailing negative EPS. Forward P/E is not meaningful in this case, however, because next year's earnings are expected to be negative.

   B. Hand has an E/P of –0.100, and Somersault has an E/P of –0.125. A higher earnings yield has an interpretation that is similar to that of a lower P/E, so Hand appears to be relatively undervalued. The difference in earnings yield cannot be explained by differences in sales growth forecasts. In fact, Hand has a higher expected sales growth rate than Somersault. Therefore, the analyst should recommend Hand.

3. A. Because investing looks to the future, analysts often favor forward P/E when earnings forecasts are available, as they are here. A specific reason to use forward P/Es is the

fact given that RUF had some unusual items affecting EPS for 2008. The data to make appropriate adjustments to RUF's 2008 EPS are not given. In summary, Stewart should use forward P/Es.

B. Because RUF has a complex capital structure, the P/Es of the two companies must be compared on the basis of diluted EPS.

   For HS, forward P/E = $44/2.20 = 20.

   For RUF, forward P/E per diluted share = $22.50/(30,000,000/33,333,333) = 25.

   Therefore, HS has the more attractive valuation at present.

   The problem illustrates some of the considerations that should be taken into account in using P/Es and the method of comparables.

4. A. Your conclusion may be in error because of the following:
   • The peer-group stocks themselves may be overvalued; that is, the mean P/E of 18 may be too high in terms of intrinsic value. If so, using 18 as a multiplier of the stock's expected EPS will lead to an estimate of stock value in excess of intrinsic value.
   • The stock's fundamentals may differ from those of the mean food-processing industry stock. For example, if the stock's expected growth rate is lower than the mean industry growth rate and its risk is higher than the mean, the stock may deserve a lower P/E than the industry mean.
   In addition, mean P/E may be influenced by outliers.

   B. The following additional evidence would support the original conclusion:
   • Evidence that stocks in the industry are, at least on average, fairly valued (that stock prices reflect fundamentals).
   • Evidence that no significant differences exist in the fundamental drivers of P/E for the stock being compared and the average industry stock.

5. In principle, the use of any price multiple for valuation is subject to the concern stated. If the stock market is overvalued, an asset that appears to be fairly valued or even under-valued in relation to an equity index may also be overvalued.

6. A. P/E for a stable-growth company is the payout ratio divided by the difference between the required rate of return and the growth rate of dividends. If the P/E is being calculated on trailing earnings (year 0), the payout ratio is increased by 1 plus the growth rate. According to the 2007 income statement, the payout ratio is 18/60 = 0.30; the 2008 income statement gives the same number (24/80 = 0.30). Thus, the P/E based on trailing earnings is

$$P/E = [\text{Payout ratio} \times (1 + g)]/(r - g)$$
$$= (0.30 \times 1.13)/(0.14 - 0.13) = 33.9$$

The P/E based on next year's earnings is

$$P/E = \text{Payout ratio}/(r - g) = 0.30/(0.14 - 0.13) = 30$$

B.

Fundamental Factor	Effect on P/E	Explanation (not required in question)
The risk (beta) of Sundanci increases substantially.	Decrease	P/E is a decreasing function of risk—that is, as risk increases, P/E decreases. Increases in the risk of Sundanci stock would be expected to lower its P/E.

The estimated growth rate of Sundanci's earnings and dividends increases.	Increase	P/E is an increasing function of the growth rate of the company—that is, the higher the expected growth, the higher the P/E. Sundanci would command a higher P/E if the market price were to incorporate expectations of a higher growth rate.
The equity risk premium increases.	Decrease	P/E is a decreasing function of the equity risk premium. An increased equity risk premium increases the required rate of return, which lowers the price of a stock relative to its earnings. A higher equity risk premium would be expected to lower Sundanci's P/E.

7. A. V_n = Benchmark value of P/E $\times E_n$ = 12 $\times$ \$3.00 = \$36.0.

   B. In the expression for sustainable growth rate $g = b \times$ ROE, you can use $(1 - 0.45) = 0.55 = b$, and ROE = 0.10 (the industry average), obtaining 0.55 $\times$ 0.10 = 0.055. Given the required rate of return of 0.09, you obtain the estimate \$3.00(0.45)(1.055)/(0.09 − 0.055) = \$40.69. In this case, the estimate of terminal value obtained from the Gordon growth model is higher than the estimate based on multiples. The two estimates may differ for a number of reasons, including the sensitivity of the Gordon growth model to the values of the inputs.

8. Although the measurement of book value has a number of widely recognized shortcomings, P/B may still be applied fruitfully in several circumstances:

   • The company is not expected to continue as a going concern. When a company is likely to be liquidated (so ongoing earnings and cash flow are not relevant), the value of its assets less its liabilities is of utmost importance. Naturally, the analyst must establish the fair value of these assets.

   • The company is composed mainly of liquid assets, which is the case for finance, investment, insurance, and banking institutions.

   • The company's EPS is highly variable or negative.

9. A. Aratatech: P/S = (\$10 price per share)/[(\$1 billion sales)/(20 million shares)] = \$10/(\$1,000,000,000/20,000,000) = 0.2

   Trymye: P/S = (\$20 price per share)/[(\$1.6 billion sales)/(30 million shares)] = \$20/(\$1,600,000,000/30,000,000) = 0.375

   Aratatech has a more attractive valuation than Trymye based on its lower P/S but comparable profit margin.

   B. One advantage of P/S over P/E is that companies' accounting decisions typically have a much greater impact on reported earnings than they are likely to have on reported sales. Although companies are able to make a number of legitimate business and accounting decisions that affect earnings, their discretion over reported sales (revenue recognition) is limited. Another advantage is that sales are almost always positive, so using P/S eliminates issues that arise when EPS is zero or negative.

10. A. The P/Es are

Hoppelli	25.70/1.30 = 19.8
Telli	11.77/0.40 = 29.4
Drisket	23.65/1.14 = 20.7
Whiteline	24.61/2.43 = 10.1

The EV/S multiples for each company are

Hoppelli	3,779/4,124 = 0.916
Telli	4,056/10,751 = 0.377
Drisket	3,846/17,388 = 0.221
Whiteline	4,258/6,354 = 0.670

B. The data for the problem include measures of profitability, such as operating profit margin, ROE, and net profit margin. Because EV includes the market values of both debt and equity, logically the ranking based on EV/S should be compared with a pre-interest measure of profitability, namely, operating profit margin. The ranking of the stocks by EV/S from highest to lowest and the companies' operating margins are:

Company	EV/S	Operating Profit Margin
Hoppelli	0.916	6.91%
Whiteline	0.670	6.23%
Telli	0.377	1.26%
Drisket	0.221	1.07%

The differences in EV/S appear to be explained, at least in part, by differences in cost structure as measured by operating profit margin.

11. For companies in the industry described, EV/S would be superior to either of the other two ratios. Among other considerations, EV/S is
   • More useful than P/E in valuing companies with negative earnings.
   • Better than either P/E or P/B for comparing companies in different countries that are likely to use different accounting standards (a consequence of the multinational nature of the industry).
   • Less subject to manipulation than earnings (i.e., through aggressive accounting decisions by management, who may be more motivated to manage earnings when a company is in a cyclical low, rather than in a high, and thus likely to report losses).

12. A. Based on the CAPM, the required rate of return is 4.9% + 1.2 × 5.5% = 11.5%.
   B. The dividend payout ratio is €0.91/€1.36 = 0.669. The justified values for the three valuation ratios should be

$$\frac{P_0}{E_0} = \frac{(1-b) \times (1+g)}{r-g} = \frac{0.669 \times 1.09}{0.115 - 0.09} = \frac{0.7293}{0.025} = 29.2$$

$$\frac{P_0}{B_0} = \frac{ROE - g}{r-g} = \frac{0.27 - 0.09}{0.115 - 0.09} = \frac{0.18}{0.025} = 7.2$$

$$\frac{P_0}{S_0} = \frac{PM \times (1-b) \times (1+g)}{r-g} = \frac{0.1024 \times 0.669 \times 1.09}{0.115 - 0.09} = \frac{0.0747}{0.025} = 3.0$$

C. The justified trailing P/E is higher than the trailing P/E (29.2 versus 28.3), the justified P/B is higher than the actual P/B (7.2 versus 7.1), and the justified P/S is higher than the actual P/S (3.0 versus 2.9). Therefore, based on these three measures, GG appears to be slightly undervalued.

13. A. EBITDA = Net income (from continuing operations) + Interest expense + Taxes + Depreciation + Amortization

   EBITDA for RGI = €49.5 million + €3 million + €2 million + €8 million
                  = €62.5 million
   Per-share EBITDA = (€62.5 million)/(5 million shares) = €12.5
   P/EBITDA for RGI = €150/€12.5 = 12

   EBITDA for NCI = €8 million + €5 million + €3 million + €4 million = €20 million
   Per-share EBITDA = (€20 million)/(2 million shares) = €10
   P/EBITDA for NCI = €100/€10 = 10

   B. For RGI:

   $$\text{Market value of equity} = €150 \times 5 \text{ million} = €750 \text{ million}$$
   $$\text{Market value of debt} = €50$$
   $$\text{Total market value} = €750 \text{ million} + €50 = €800 \text{ million}$$

   $$EV = €800 \text{ million} - €5 \text{ million (cash and investments)} = €795 \text{ million}$$

   Now, Zaldys would divide EV by total (as opposed to per-share) EBITDA:

   $$\text{EV/EBITDA for RGI} = (€795 \text{ million})/(€62.5 \text{ million}) = 12.72$$

   For NCI:

   $$\text{Market value of equity} = €100 \times 2 \text{ million} = €200 \text{ million}$$
   $$\text{Market value of debt} = €100$$
   $$\text{Total market value} = €200 \text{ million} + €100 = €300 \text{ million}$$

   $$EV = €300 \text{ million} - €2 \text{ million (cash and investments)} = €298 \text{ million}$$

   Now, Zaldys would divide EV by total (as opposed to per-share) EBITDA:

   $$\text{EV/EBITDA for NCI} = (€298 \text{ million})/(€20 \text{ million}) = 14.9$$

   C. Zaldys should select RGI as relatively undervalued.
   First, it is correct that NCI *appears* to be relatively undervalued based on P/EBITDA, because NCI has a lower P/EBITDA multiple:

   - P/EBITDA = €150/€12.5 = 12 for RGI
   - P/EBITDA = €100/€10 = 10 for NCI

   RGI is relatively undervalued on the basis of EV/EBITDA, however, because RGI has the lower EV/EBITDA multiple:

   - EV/EBITDA = (€795 million)/(€62.5 million) = 12.72 for RGI
   - EV/EBITDA = (€298 million)/(€20 million) = 14.9 for NCI

       EBITDA is a pre-interest flow; therefore, it is a flow to both debt and equity and the EV/EBITDA multiple is more appropriate than the P/EBITDA multiple.

Zaldys would rely on EV/EBITDA to reach his decision if the two ratios conflicted. Note that P/EBITDA does not take into account differences in the use of financial leverage. Substantial differences in leverage exist in this case (NCI uses much more debt), so the preference for using EV/EBITDA rather than P/EBITDA is supported.

14. The major concepts are as follows:
   - EPS plus per-share depreciation, amortization, and depletion (CF)
     Limitation: Ignores changes in working capital and noncash revenue; not a free cash flow concept.
   - Cash flow from operations (CFO)
     Limitation: Not a free cash flow concept, so not directly linked to theory.
   - Free cash flow to equity (FCFE)
     Limitation: Often more variable and more frequently negative than other cash flow concepts.
   - Earnings before interest, taxes, depreciation, and amortization (EBITDA)
     Limitation: Ignores changes in working capital and noncash revenue; not a free cash flow concept. Relative to its use in P/EBITDA, EBITDA is mismatched with the numerator because it is a pre-interest concept.

15. MAT Technology is relatively undervalued compared with DriveMed on the basis of P/FCFE. MAT Tech's P/FCFE multiple is 34 percent the size of DriveMed's FCFE multiple (15.6/46 = 0.34, or 34 percent). The only comparison slightly in DriveMed's favor, or approximately equal for both companies, is the comparison based on P/CF (i.e., 12.8 for DriveMed versus 13.0 for MAT Technology). However, FCFE is more strongly grounded in valuation theory than P/CF. Because DriveMed's and MAT Technology's expenditures for fixed capital and working capital during the previous year reflected anticipated average expenditures over the foreseeable horizon, you would have additional confidence in the P/FCFE comparison.

16. A. Relative strength is based strictly on price movement (a technical indicator). As used by Westard, the comparison is between the returns on HCI and the returns on the S&P 500. In contrast, the price multiple approaches are based on the relationship of current price, not to past prices, but to some measure of value such as EPS, book value, sales, or cash flow.

    B. Only the reference to the P/E in relationship to the pending patent applications in Westard's recommendation is consistent with the company's value orientation. High relative strength would be relevant for a portfolio managed with a growth/momentum investment style.

17. A. As a rule, a screen that includes a maximum P/E ratio should include criteria requiring positive earnings; otherwise, the screen could select companies with negative P/E ratios. The screen may be too narrowly focused on value measures. It did not include criteria related to expected growth, required rate of return, risk, or financial strength.

    B. The screen results in a very concentrated portfolio. The screen selected both of the parent companies of the Unilever Group: Unilever NV and Unilever PLC, which operate as a single business entity despite having separate legal identities and separate stock exchange listings. Thus, owning both stocks would provide no diversification benefits. In addition, the screen selected three tobacco companies, which typically pay high dividends. Again, owning all three stocks would provide little diversification.

CHAPTER 7

PRIVATE COMPANY VALUATION

SOLUTIONS

1. A strategic buyer seeks to eliminate unnecessary expenses. The strategic buyer would adjust the reported EBITDA by the amount of the officers' excess compensation. A strategic buyer could also eliminate redundant manufacturing costs estimated at £600,000. The pro forma EBITDA a strategic buyer might use in its acquisition analysis is the reported EBITDA of £4,500,000 plus the nonmarket compensation expense of £500,000 plus the operating synergies (cost savings) of £600,000. The adjusted EBITDA for the strategic buyer is £4,500,000 + £500,000 + £600,000 = £5,600,000. The financial buyer would also make the adjustment to normalize officers' compensation but would not be able to eliminate redundant manufacturing expenses. Thus, adjusted EBITDA for the financial buyer would be £4,500,000 + £500,000 = £5,000,000.

2. The build-up method is substantially similar to the extended CAPM except that beta is excluded from the calculation. The equity return requirement is calculated as risk-free rate plus equity risk premium for large capitalization stocks plus small stock risk premium plus company-specific risk premium: 4.5 + 5.0 + 4.2 + 3.0 = 16.7 percent. Although practice may vary, in this case, there was no adjustment for industry risk.

3. There are FCFF and FCFE variations of the CCM. In this problem, the data permit the application of just the FCFE variation. According to that variation, the estimated value of equity equals the normalized free cash flow to equity estimate for next period divided by the capitalization rate for equity. The capitalization rate is the required rate of return for equity less the long-term growth rate in free cash flow to equity. Using the current $1.8 million of free cash flow to equity, the 18 percent equity discount rate, and the long-term growth rate of 5.5 percent yields a value indication of [($1.8 million)(1.055)]/(0.18 − 0.055) = $1.899 million/0.125 = $15.19 million.

4. The excess earnings consist of any remaining income after returns to working capital and fixed assets are considered. Fair value estimates and rate of return requirements for working capital and fixed assets are provided. The return required for working capital is $2,000,000 × 5.0 percent = $100,000 and the return required for fixed assets is $5,500,000 × 8.0 percent = $440,000, or $540,000 in total.

This chapter was contributed by Raymond D. Rath, ASA, CFA.

A. The residual income for intangible assets is $460,000 (the normalized earnings of $1,000,000 less the $540,000 required return for working capital and intangible assets). The value of intangible assets can then be calculated using the capitalized cash flow method. The intangibles value is $4,600,000 based on $460,000 of income available to the intangibles capitalized at 10.0 percent (15.0 percent discount rate for intangibles less 5.0 percent long-term growth rate).

B. The market value of invested capital is the total of the values of working capital, fixed assets, and intangible assets. This value is $2,000,000 + $5,500,000 + $4,830,000 = $12,330,000.

5. The valuation of a small equity interest in a private company would typically be calculated on a basis that reflects the lack of control and lack of marketability of the interest. The control premium of 15 percent must first be used to provide an indication of a discount for lack of control (DLOC). A lack of control discount can be calculated using the formula

$$\text{Lack of control discount} = 1 - [1/ (1 + \text{Control premium})]$$

In this case, a lack of control discount of approximately 13 percent is calculated as 1– [1/(1 + 15%)]. The discount for lack of marketability (DLOM) was specified. Valuation discounts are applied sequentially and are not added. The formula is

$$(\text{Pro rata control value}) \times (1 - \text{DLOC}) \times (1 - \text{DLOM})$$

A combined discount of approximately 35 percent is calculated as $1 - (1 - 13\%) \times (1 - 25\%) = 0.348$ or 34.8 percent.

6. A is correct. Both the current shareholders and the future shareholders (the private investment group) share the same expectations. It is most reasonable to assume that both are concerned with Thunder's intrinsic value, which market prices should reflect when the company is brought public under less volatile market conditions.

7. B is correct. The size of Thunder and its probable lack of access to public debt markets are potential factors affecting the valuation of Thunder compared with a public company. Given that the separation of ownership and control at Thunder is similar to that at public companies, however, agency problems are not a distinguishing factor in its valuation.

8. C is correct. The excess earnings method would rarely be applied to value the equity of a company particularly when it is not needed to value intangibles. The asset-based approach is less appropriate because it is infrequently used to estimate the business enterprise value of operating companies. By contrast, the free cash flow method is broadly applicable and readily applied in this case.

9. A is correct. Using Ebinosa's assumptions:

Revenues ($200,000,000 x 1.03 =)		$206,000,000
Gross profit	45%[a]	92,700,000
Selling, general, and administrative expenses	24%[a]	49,440,000
Pro forma EBITDA		43,260,000
Depreciation	2%[a]	4,120,000

Pro forma EBIT		39,140,000
Pro forma taxes on EBIT	35%[b]	13,699,000
Operating income after tax		$25,441,000
Plus: Depreciation		4,120,000
Less: Capital expenditures on current sales	125%[c]	5,150,000
Less: Capital expenditures to support future sales	15%[d]	900,000
Less: Working capital requirement	8%[d]	480,000
Free cash flow to the firm		$23,031,000

[a]Percent of revenues
[b]Percent of EBIT
[c]Percent of depreciation
[d]Percent of incremental revenues.

10. C is correct. Both statements by Chin are incorrect. If the CAPM is used with public companies with similar operations and similar revenue size, as stated, then the calculation likely captures the small stock premium and should not be added to the estimate. Small stock premiums are associated with build-up models and the expanded CAPM, rather than the CAPM per se. The correct weighted average cost of capital should reflect the risk of Thunder's cash flows, not the risk of the acquirer's cash flows.

11. A is correct. The return on equity is the sum of the risk-free rate, equity risk premium, and the size premium for a total of $4.5 + 5.0 + 2.0 = 11.5$ percent. The value of the firm using the CCM is $V = FCFE_1/(r - g) = 2.5/(0.115 - 0.03) = \$29.41$ million.

12. B is correct. Oakstar's primary asset is timberland whose market value can be determined from comparable land sales.

13. B is correct. In the absence of market value data for assets and liabilities, the analyst usually must use book value data (the text explicitly makes the assumption that book values accurately reflect market values as well). Except for timberland, market values for assets are not available. Thus, all other assets are assumed to be valued by their book values, which sum to $\$500,000 + \$25,000 + \$50,000 + \$750,000 = \$1,325,000$. The value of the land is determined by the value of $\$8,750$ per hectare for properties comparable to Oakstar's. Thus, the value of Oakstar's land is $\$8,750 \times 10,000 = \$87,500,000$. Liabilities are assumed to be worth the sum of their book value or $\$1,575,000$. Thus, Estimated value = Total assets − Liabilities = $\$1,325,000 + \$87,500,000 - \$1,575,000 = \$87,250,000$.

14. C is correct. The new interest level is $\$2,000,000$ instead of $\$1,000,000$. SG&A expenses are reduced by $\$1,600,000 (= \$5,400,000 - \$7,000,000)$ to $\$21,400,000$ by salary expense savings. Other than a calculation of a revised provision for taxes, no other changes to the income statement results in normalized earnings before tax of $\$58,100,000$ and normalized earnings after tax of $\$34,860,000$.

15. B is correct:

    Return on working capital $= 0.08 \times \$10,000,000 = \$800,000$
    Return on fixed assets $= 0.12 \times \$45,000,000 = \$5,400,000$
    Return on intangibles $= \$35,000,000 - \$800,000 - \$5,400,000 = \$28,800,000$
    Value of intangibles using CCM $= \$28,800,000/(0.20 - 0.06) = \$205.71$ million.

16. C is correct. Firm 3 matches FAMCO in both risk and growth. Firm 1 fails on these factors. In addition, Firm 3 is a better match to FAMCO than Firm 2 because the offer for Firm 3 was a cash offer in normal market conditions whereas Firm 2 was a stock offer in a boom market and the value does not reflect risk and growth in the immediate future.

17. B is correct. Both discounts apply and they are multiplicative rather than additive: $1 - (1 - 0.20)(1 - 0.15) = 1 - 0.68 = 32$ percent.

ABOUT THE CFA PROGRAM

The Chartered Financial Analyst® designation (CFA®) is a globally recognized standard of excellence for measuring the competence and integrity of investment professionals. To earn the CFA charter, candidates must successfully pass through the CFA Program, a global graduate-level self-study program that combines a broad curriculum with professional conduct requirements as preparation for a wide range of investment specialties.

Anchored by a practice-based curriculum, the CFA Program is focused on the knowledge identified by professionals as essential to the investment decision-making process. This body of knowledge maintains current relevance through a regular, extensive survey of practicing CFA charterholders across the globe. The curriculum covers 10 general topic areas, ranging from equity and fixed-income analysis to portfolio management to corporate finance, all with a heavy emphasis on the application of ethics in professional practice. Known for its rigor and breadth, the CFA Program curriculum highlights principles common to every market so that professionals who earn the CFA designation have a thoroughly global investment perspective and a profound understanding of the global marketplace.

www.cfainstitute.org

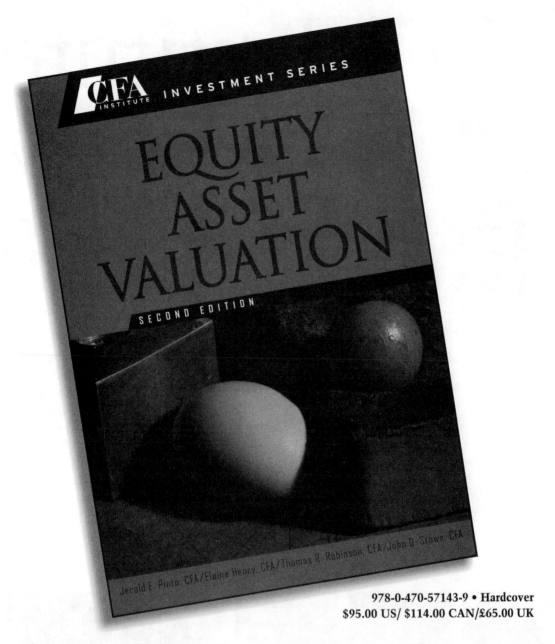

978-0-470-57143-9 • Hardcover
$95.00 US/ $114.00 CAN/£65.00 UK

Discover the distinct methods of **equity asset valuation** from some of the best minds in the business.

CFA Institute
+ Wiley
= Success

978-0-470-57143-9
Hardcover
$95.00 US
$114.00 CAN
£65.00 UK

978-0-470-39521-9
Paper
$39.95 US
$47.95 CAN
£26.99 UK

John Wiley & Sons and CFA Institute are proud to present the *CFA Institute Investment Series* geared specifically for industry professionals and graduate-level students. This cutting-edge series focuses on the most important topics in the finance industry. The authors of these books are themselves leading industry professionals and academics who bring their wealth of knowledge and expertise to you.

Clear, example-driven coverage of a wide range of valuation, investment risk, and quantitative finance methods is the hallmark feature of every title in this new series.

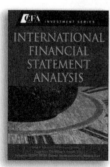

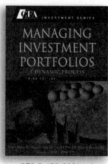

978-0-470-05221-1	978-0-470-28766-8	978-0-470-08014-6	978-0-470-05220-4	978-0-470-19768-4
Hardcover • $95.00 US	Hardcover • $95.00 US	Hardcover • $95.00 US	Hardcover • $95.00 US	Hardcover • $95.95 US
$114.00 CAN/£65.00 UK	$114.00 CAN/£65.00 UK	$114.00 CAN/£65.00 UK	$114.00 CAN/£65.00 UK	$120.95 CAN/£49.99 UK

WILEY

Now you know.

wiley.com

Available at wiley.com, cfainstitute.org, and wherever books are sold.